Robin Morgan's first volu
Monster, was well received fo
complishment and became a

ROBIN MORGAN has bee

by ROBIN MORGAN

~ ~ ~ ~

POETRY

Monster

Lady of the Beasts

NONFICTION

Going Too Far

ANTHOLOGY

Sisterhood is Powerful (ed.)

LADY OF THE BEASTS

Lady of the Beasts

~~~~~~~~~~~~~~~~~~~~~~~~~~~~~~~~~~

poems by ROBIN MORGAN

~~~~~~~~~~~~~~~~~~~~~~~~~~~~~~~~~~

 RANDOM HOUSE • NEW YORK

Some of the poems in this book have appeared in: *Amazon Quarterly,
Chomo Uri, The Common Woman, Moving Out, Ms., Poetry North-
west, The Sewanee Review, Sojourner,* and *Sunbury.*

"The Network of the Imaginary Mother," the long poem which com-
prises Part VI of this volume, first appeared in *The American Poetry
Review.*

The author gratefully acknowledges permission to quote from *The Great
Mother* by Erich Neumann, translated by Ralph Manheim, Bollingen
Series XLVII (Copyright © 1955 by The Bollingen Foundation). Re-
printed by permission of Princeton University Press.

DESIGN BY ANTONINA KRASS

Library of Congress Cataloging in Publication Data
Morgan, Robin
Lady of the beasts.
I. T.
PS3563. O87148L3
1976
811'.5'4   76-10750
ISBN 0-394-40758-X
ISBN 0-39473299-4 PBK

MANUFACTURED IN THE UNITED STATES OF AMERICA
2 3 4 5 6 7 8 9
FIRST EDITION

Woman was entrusted with the care of the captive young animals; she was the tamer of domestic beasts and the founder of cattle breeding. What is more, she domesticated the male through the taboos that she imposed on him, and so created the first human culture. In exacting the domination, curtailment, and sacrifice of the instinctual drives, the Lady of the Beasts represented more than the principle of natural order. She was more than a protectress and breeder of beasts.

Thus the formative power of the Feminine that is realized in this connection starts from the narrowest confines of the family, tribe, or clan. But here it does not remain; in the course of human development it achieves transformations that show why the supreme embodiments of the Great Goddess always reflect woman's ability and willingness to love. For neither the exaction of sacrifice nor domination over the world of plants and animals, the instinctual world of the unconscious, is the central concern of the Great Goddess. Over both these stands the law of transformation in which she sublimates all life and raises it to a development where, without losing its bond with the root and foundation, it achieves the highest forms of psychic reality.

—Erich Neumann,
The Great Mother

CONTENTS

1

~~~~~~~~~~~~~

BLOOD TIES

LOYALTY OATH

Ungrateful Daughter, Intolerant Friend,
Officious Associate, Malcontent Wife:
these signs, hand-lettered in uneven print.
The oppressed carry them around inside my skull
in shifts. They want to organize,
despite my efforts to negotiate
an individual settlement with each.

Even in darkness, barred from sleep
by their chanting, I know I must break that union
or turn hopeless, mad, intransigent—no,
that's another lie. Management
has botched the whole thing, all along.
Yet to see each such lunatic as unrelated
to the fringe would be a self-deception.

What are they protesting? I only obeyed orders
we gave each other; in fact, followed policies
I never wished to formulate. And long ago tried pacifying,
at random, one dissenter—to find such tactics merely
brought more rabble to the gates. I pass out leaflets
gravely listing all my domino excuses:
self-preservation, commitment, professionality, naiveté.

These go unread by the illiterate protesters.
They are hardly aware of each other, of their own litanies,
and absurdly unmoved by the coffee and sandwiches I send them.
How dare they refuse to settle with me?
I have loved those they claim to represent.
I am owed something.
Who do they think has kept them alive all this time?

See, that old woman whose accusing tears
glow like pearls sewn to her sable jacket,

the fur bought by my childish labor, the tears in payment
for my maturation. And that old man goose-stepping
arrogantly by, flanked by his precious sons—what interest
do I owe such parents who never quite invested
in their child one glance between possession and indifference?

And there, that group with pained, intelligent expressions
and idle hands spotless of ink, paint, blood,
or any brave stain I could infect them with,
disclaiming an envy no abasement of mine would ever ease.
Or look at those who drag their banners, light up cigarettes,
and gossip even at the dedication of their comrades.
They say I should picket for them; I'd do it better.

Now that man all alone, though—he's impressive:
completely naked except for scars he and I carved
together—lovers' initials on a living tree.
He's reasonable, as well, offering to mediate
between me and the others. He even smiles and waves
sometimes, or is that merely pragmatism?
He marches out there still.

At this age surely one half the wait is over.
But if already they have struck with such effectiveness—
a wildcat slowdown of my body, my mind
unable to promote its image, my words pressed
into employment on this page to stutter lies more radical
than any truths—how can this deadlock be resolved
when each year newer converts join their protest?

Even now, an in-depth guilt-survey can prophesy
fresh posters readied, unlegended but grained
with photographs of babies starving in five-color separation,
of un-class-conscious students, of workers justified
in beating up their wives, of miserly redwoods—each tree
hoarding a whole development of Leisure Villages,
of rapists I should try to understand

and victims I must emulate correctly,
and one last black-and-white collectively created graphic:
a bonfire purifying poems of their irrelevance.
Pity, self- or otherwise, scabs the heart at last.
I'd go insane if that would do the trick.
But I'd need them for that, to riot and seize my brain
entirely—and they are not adventuristic opportunists.

I'd kill myself, but they, you see, are unprepared
for self-determination. Someone has to be responsible.
So we wait our revolution out. They give me my small comforts.
They let me write. They help me with my choice of words.
They dictated this, in fact—which means it might get published
and maybe even read by you
as evidence.

THE FATHER

"Girls of your age are the freshest, purest things
    Our Blessed Lord has made."
  I was just twelve, and fatherless.
    The winter carousel
in Central Park was ours. I drank hot chocolate,
    he chain-smoked cigarettes.
  Books, relics, blessings warmed me
    less than his smell, of lime
and incense. I was not Catholic, but he still
    held me on his lap,
  and sent me flowers on Father's Day.

    He was new in my world of women;
my mother and aunts thought him strange but safe,
    and useful to our needs.
  I wrote him letters every day,
    learned Latin with delight,
spent weekends with his parents in the country.
    His mother had been dying
  since his birth; for forty years
    she thrived, patient to outlive
her husband, take sole possession of their son.
    His father told Irish jokes
  and felt between my legs to warn
    me not to let boys touch there.
He never did that. Often we didn't touch
    at all, but sat and watched
  the space that breathed between our hands.
    He said I would outgrow him,
and every birthday, teased my bitterness
    at others who, he smiled,
  had gone before me, and would follow.
    He asked for the frock I had worn
the day we met, and folded it in a box

tied with satin ribbon,
to remember me as a child, I thought.
He called me Princess.
Once, he was drunk, and slapped me in the face.

Years later, married and pregnant,
I saw them in the park one summer afternoon,
his collar cast away
beside her shoes and socks. Her pinafore was stained.
Surprising them, I loomed, a green
round shadow against the sun, and laughed
"You don't know me!" but pity
stung my eyes at her protective anger
for him who, kneeling on the grass,
looked as if he saw heat shimmering with some
dreaded annunciation.

THE VOYEUR

In counterpointed quarrel they play,
trading the victim's and the victor's roles,
I focus on the score, eager to seize
a cadence beyond my view: the harmony
    I know, offstage, their silences complete.

Within my walls their voices hum;
their angry figures (slitted by the blind
that with the darkened lamp protects my breed)
deceive me. Their bed is in a farther room.
    But they include me in their hate.

Etched on my glass, those furies move
alien to their later, sheeted guise.
Who but a saint would hallow in his praise
temptations he rejects in his dim cave
    but needs, to stay inviolate?

They reconcile. Betrayed, my role
is now to strain, a mute within a choir
who mouths dumb hallelujahs, safe to discover
none of his silence for the easy swell
    of song that fills his neighbor's throat.

I lose them to that other room
where damned and celebrating still, they gesture.
I draw my blinds against them, but I fear
my body lying open to their rhythms,
    their negative still seared upon my sight.

THE COVENANT
(for K.P.)

I see them live behind your gaze—
sister and father, wraithful pair—
and watch you sweat to synthesize
or rend them, year on haunted year.
You, their prison and battlefield,
brother and son who could not cure
the martyr's zeal when once it kindled
the executioner's slow fire.

I feel my vision darken, too:
phantoms lust to breathe our fear.
That pulsing double shape I know;
longing embowels me—I, the liar
who never loved the father-ghost
smiling from masks you never wore.
Your specters age with salted rust
but mine run fresh blood everywhere.

I know how well you loved the maid
who shared that grim paternity—
who died, and rose again, and died
with many men, trusting the lie
her father told her when he slew
her angels. Those same angels bind me

to your suffering now.
My father's lips move when you pray.

Bodies, to brave what dreams dare show,
must recognize each faceless ghost.
Give me my father. I give you
your sister, and procure her rest
from wanting him. So we fulfill
their final promise with our first—
and you and I, who share this hell,
again lose what was always lost.

LOVE POEM OF THE CALENDAR ALPHABET

[In its content, metaphor, and metrics, this poem reflects the
structural, symbolic, and numerological values of the ancient
Celtic Beth-Luis-Nion Tree Alphabet, as explicated by Robert
Graves in *The White Goddess*.]

Birch-bright are these bodies,
        cradling our newborn selves.

Like lightning you impale my heart's red berry;
        I study the oracular entrails, still smoking
        grey as a rowan fire.

Nursing each other with sweat clear as the snipe's song,
        we would drown but for these egos—stout oars of ash;
        We are left flooded, silt-fertile.

Fire spirals from us as from hewn alderwood,
        whistling like a crimson gull.

Sifting apart, we fall, lost grains through wicker sieves;
        the moon owns me, I grieve where the willow mourns,
        and yours is the hawk's trial: insight and despair.

Zygotic lover I labor, repeating you
        as the thrush stutters the rainbow:
        Behold my staff. Where I have struck
        or leaned on you, you put forth leaves.

Hold me chastely, as the night-crow grasps terror;
        nothing has any value.

Desperate, we signal across two needfires; we are naive
        midsummer wrens, battering the door between us.

Twin, which of us is sacrificed? I, the arch, the altar?
        or you who cling there, blossoming?

Concentrate of each other in one shell, we solve
> the crane's asymmetry.

Quince be your canopy, the garden your refuge,
> the unasked question your tether.
> I peck at the gleaned field.

Maenad that I am,
> I thirst for your vintage self.

Gates open in me; now would I resurrect you
> with that love which strikes the blue swan mute.

Gnostic geese, we who dwell empowered
> under one roof.

Ripening well into winter, we may yet learn
> how our roots entwine and drink at one source:
> an elder wisdom, therapeutic, a mutual doom.

And yet, alone, each of us thrived in salt-charged sand;
> I had no brother who sought me, as you did
> your sister—or am I silvering through her mirror,
> a lost Tamar myself, thinking I seek my son?

Our histories are being burnt away, like furze
> singed to clear space for fresh sprouts' greening;
> we sense our own preparedness for this buzz,
> electricate, in our touch.

Uproarious
> at last as mountain heather, we arrive;
> you are drenched larkspur by this passion
> and I am dry of wing—ready, now, to hive.

Entropy, we know, consumes all our consuming, will blaze us
> and then bury us—but upright in our graves

if we have earned it, like poplars
exuberant on a darkening autumn hill.

I will not love you then, nor will you care for me,
        despite all our intentions—except as our dead mouths
        may speak roots subtler than these tongues:
        poems probing through the earth-dull ears of others,
        gnarling into a single trunk, an utterance.

Joined at such a height,
        we gaze at one another undisguised—
        this risk dangerous as a fall
        toward no certain ground;
        this space massing white as distance
        which shreds, powerless,
        before the glance of
        eagles such as we.

II

~~~~~~~~~~~~~~

THE CITY OF GOD

THE CITY OF GOD

(in memoriam Milena Jesenská)

"Can one be a saint without God? That's
the problem, in fact the only problem."
 —Albert Camus, *The Plague*

I just got up. Incredible. I just got up
and lurched downstairs to put on water for tea
and wait for it to boil.
But I am the one who is simmering
already, and my god, I just got up.

What a cosmic error,
to have decided to sit at the kitchen table
and wait for the water to boil.
Look at the cockroach egg laid precisely
in the crack between the table leaves.
Another member of the colony is crawling up one chairleg,
having heard, no doubt, about the crumbheaps
left in the tufts of the chair cushions
whenever the four-year-old passes through.
Lower-east-side ninety-five-degree Manhattan July
lies flat in the rooms, not even air enough to stir
the coy dustballs nestled in corners,
under the furniture, in the crotch of each stairstep.
No Saint Elmo's Fire here,
but filth enough to cause Saint Jerome
nine mystical orgasms.

I try looking up, away—another mistaken assumption, embodying
only the ceiling. Low anyway as the New York smog,
it chuggles cracked plaster, peeling paint,
discolorations, across my gaze.
Not to speak of the moon craters,
holes the size of my clenched fist

left there from the last time we tore down a wall.
It was to give the illusion of greater space;
time being what it is, the holes remain,
now and then belching little chunklets of plaster
or an exposed beam's offsprung splinter down,
like mini-inverted volcanoes, extinct we imagine,
reminding us of their presence
in the blank, skun face of heaven.

There are holes in the face of hell too, of course:
jagged chasms leering between the antique floorboards,
gorges which have been patched and filled so many times,
only to warp again at the slightest weight.
Cockroaches crawl amicably up through them, and lately
giant water beetles—they're a treat only Saint Francis could love.
I start to meditate on whether the downstairs cockroaches
have met their brothers upstairs, whether each has some intimation
that there are comrades near, or not.
I wonder if it would be kind
to bring one of these from the table to meet a sister by the sink,
or to transport three or four—a small collective—
to parley with the batch upstairs. But which batch?
Elitist of me to choose.

After all, there are roaches in the child's room,
reeling like science-fiction monsters
through the doll-house doors;
intellectual roaches who patrol the chessboard,
music lovers who jostle the wires and wheels of the phonograph
(which is of course unplayable and a cast-of-thousands production
to get fixed, dear Jude, patron of hopeless projects).
There are the roaches who dart insectual advances
at my sleeping body, on those memorable nights
when I bound out of bed, sweating,
to shudder them off—factual visitations
more ingenious than my nightmares.
Do these comprise the phallus of their lord, Theresa?
When I light the oven, infrequently in summer,

roaches run from all the burners
like Albigensians scurrying, singed, from the fire.
I wish their reproductive habits were as chaste.
There was one frozen to death on the lowest refrigerator shelf,
next to something left uncovered, rotting.
No wonder you hunger-struck, Ms. Weil.
There was one in a glass of wine I had stupidly left
standing for half an hour, floating feet up
like a happy, dead Li Po.
There was an egg-sac affixed to a sheaf of my poems yesterday.
Meanwhile, my frenzied spraying merely
mutates their species, poisons our lungs.

Not that I want to be obsessed with roaches.
They are, after all, only one familiar symptom
of the malaise I sicken and die of, this one-dimensional
city summer of 1973, everything flat as a bad painting.
The money-worries, for instance,
which make me feel that poor, desperate Iscariot
was royally had.
Or the door on the downstairs cabinet
which falls on your foot when you unforgettingly swing it open,
or the clutter of errands undone:
shoes that need gluing, the faucet oozing
rust over an intrepidly stained tub, the grit on the windowsills,
the windowframes that stick and slant
like a Dr. Caligari set or a vision of Saint Dymphna's.
Small comfort, that I vow the next time anyone pontificates
a correct line on poverty and privilege to me
they will get smashed on their downwardly mobile nose.

What *about* the windows, the panes themselves,
given up on, given over to dirt,
all but opaque with grime, except where streaked
by pigeon crap, or my small son's hieroglyphic alphabet?
What good would it do to wash them and look through?
I have been there, I know what is there:
the whores shaking like saplings under a winter wind

in the blast of July, for a fix?
The pimps modeling patent leather and white linen?
The human shit on the sidewalk, pillowing the drunk
who speaks his dreams aloud in gape-mouthed mumbles?

Last week, in the bus, I was preoccupied with feet.
So many were in sandals, almost squinting
at a light they rarely see.
One woman's toes, grotesque contortions cramped beneath
a brave façade of purple polish—
I missed my stop, with staring.
Who could heal such feet?

Not to speak of Mao Tse-tung's alarm
that Watergate is hurting Nixon's reputation.
Or of my ill and aging mother now having to pay
the interest of her last years caring for a husband,
a terminal cancer patient, and a cranky obnoxious old prick,
even when well. Smile
enigmatically at that, Saint Anne.
France tested a brand-new nuclear "device" last week,
drought bloats the sub-Sahara,
and India's Untouchables are being massacred anew
for their salvation.

Where do I begin, this time?
To break the inertia, find the motor, churn the woman
and the man and even the child into cheerful and frenetic action?
And if, again,
we pacified the bruised cables, patched up the holes in roof and floor,
whirled like dervishes in a holy
delirium of paint, wax, polish, soap, spray,
and took to the shoemakers, the cleaners, the repairshop
and then picked up from the shoemakers, cleaners, repairshop,
Martha, what then? Give me some helpful hints
on what revolutionary cleaning agent
could make the women on the corner break into bloom again,
rinse the bum's mouth with rosewater,

straighten and anoint those gnarled, nailpolished claws?
What can dust off my mother's life
or scrub the air shiny again?
How many locusts would feed the sub-Saharans?
What can scour the old men and teach the new ones
to pick up after themselves?
What scarf is large enough, Veronica, to take the imprint
of so many Untouched faces?
What can recycle them?

Not to speak of having contempt for my own self-pity,
drawn into the Cabrini whirlpool of others' pain.
Not to speak of being detested or trumpeted politically,
but not understood.

Not to speak.

I have utterly lost the energy they sing at me about.
My energy, my energy, how I give it to them in waves, rays,
bursts, like sunlight. Hallelujah, how they bask in it.
The sun is dying, they forget, a star in some addict's blind eye
rapidly burning itself out.
What should I fix up this time, and watch decay?

The water is almost boiling.
I can't believe it, I just got up.
Already my ribcage is cast in bronze,
the congestion in my chest literal, as if
I had swallowed a lump of sponge.
The exterminator is due around noon, but it's early yet.
The house is waking into morning sounds, tightening around me.
Doors slamming open, bureaus yawning their drawer jaws in protest,
a toilet flushing more waste toward the rivers.
A man's footsteps overhead,
a small boy's voice, complaining.
Maria, deposed and co-opted, look how my child
is growing to schools which will rob him
of whatever grace and curiosity he still wears

like the nimbus encircling your blissful infant Horus
plumped on his momma Isis' lap.

And what word could descend
to melt the silence between this man with whom I live
and me, this woman half-alive?
What blessing for his pain? No usual struggle-phase, this—
he who has also spotted god as an immense green mantis
rotating eyes unseeing over what it reaches for, uncaring.
What miracle?

The water has boiled and will crack the pot
if I don't turn it off.

Politics is not enough.
Poetry is not enough.
Nothing is not enough.

If I could smash the carapace.

Only God would be enough, and She
is constricted inside my torture-chamber ribs,
this whole planet one bubble that floats briefly
from her drowning mouth
up toward breaking.

Oh my God, if I could wholly love Thee,
wholly be Mine own, then I would not be snared
in loving all these fragments of Thee.
Let it be done, once, complete, total.
Look at Thy doorstep, Mother, Thy feet,
where I lie in all my pieces.
See the fear that streams from my bladder.
My own divinity asphyxiates within me.

Let me take myself by force, yes Heaven,
or by pity or even by patience.
But let me not remain diasporic to myself,

shards, mosaics, clues, riddles, fossils
all my loves, creations, fears, failures, triumphs.

Peel back, universe, to the slum of your meaning.
Let me recognize one other like me in the drains.
Mother, ah,
let me sleep in the buzzing breath
of Thy preoccupied embrace.

III

THE SHUTTLE

JOTTINGS OF A FEMINIST ACTIVIST

1. On Being Beset By My Enemies

> If you can't stand the heat,
> step down from the stake.

2. On Being Beset By Some Sisters

> Sororicide is powerful—
> but ultimately a diversion
> to divert us from diverting
> the diversion of our fear.

3. On Being Understood By Some Sisters

> So, then,
> humility is, after all,
> not even
> humiliating.
> I am one experiment
> of the revolution.

ON THE WATERGATE WOMEN

Maureen Dean, wearing persimmon summer silk,
sits smiling, silent, in the Senate Hearing Room.
Her eyelids droop. She must not doze.
She bolts upright.
But if she cannot doze, she finds she *thinks*.
She is the second wife.
The first says that he never lied.
The musings of the second are inadmissible.

Martha Mitchell, Cassandra by extension,
nurses the bruises from her beatings,
nurses her mind from the forced commitments,
waits at home, alone, with the terror that all her truths
will be seen as comic relief.

Dita Beard
has disappeared,
clutching the heart she was permitted to keep
alive, in payment for her scandal's death.

Rose Mary would
if she could, but she can't;
lips sealed by loyalty (for which, read: fear),
a faintly ridiculous scapegoat
as any Good Friday girl could have predicted.

The Committee wives watch their husbands on TV,
alone, preferably, so they can smile to themselves
at the righteous purity of such judges.

All the secretaries hunch at their IBM's,
snickering at the keys.
What they know could bring down the government.

The maids, the governesses, the manicurists,
the masseuses avert their eyes.
What they know could bring down the family.

The mistresses wait for their phones to ring.
Afraid to miss the call, they hurry
through their vomiting.

None of these witnesses would be believed.
Some do not believe themselves.

And Dorothy, Mrs. Howard Hunt, tucked into her coffin,
could hardly testify
to the cash, nestled in her lap like a rapist,
to the plane's dive through a bleached spring sky,
the taste of arsenic on her teeth,
the enormous dazzling wisdom that struck all her braincells
at the impact.
Her silence should bring down the nation.

But all the while, one woman, sitting alone
in rooms and corridors thick with deceit;
familiar, by now, with an unimaginable weariness,
having smiled and waved and hostessed her only life
into a numbness that cannot now recall
even the love
which was once supposed to make all this worthwhile—

having slept out summer in a wintry bed,
having borne children who were neither of them sons,
having, for years, stood at attention
so close to power, so powerless—

not, oh not
Thelma Catherine Patricia Ryan Nixon

blamed by the Right for her careful stupidity
blamed by the Middle for her cultivated dullness
blamed by the Left for her nonexistent influence
blamed by most men for being unbeautiful
blamed by some women for being broken
blamed by her daughters for their father
blamed by her husband for her cherished mis-memory of him
     as a young Quaker—

not, oh not
Thelma Catherine Patricia Ryan Nixon

who, as a young girl, loved Scarlatti,
who wanted to become an actress playing Ibsen,
who lost her own name somewhere along the way,

who now sits alone in some oversized chair,
watching with detached interest
how her sedated visions do their best
to picket before so many defilements.

This is no melodrama.
Here is no histrionic pain.

This quality of grief
could bring down
mankind.

PORTRAIT OF THE ARTIST
AS TWO YOUNG WOMEN

(for Pat Mainardi)

Old hands,
both of us,
at consciousness-raising sessions,
at organizing, and at our respective crafts,
and old acquaintances—
we've both returned,
not having really left, to this:

You paint my portrait
while I sit for you,
writing a poem in my head
about your painting me writing.

Old hands, both of us,
we cannot help but try
to raise each other's consciousness,
reorganize each other.

You care for the pigments themselves.
Your glance quickens the practiced brush,
streaking my eyes and hair
in umbers and siennas, both raw and burnt.
You mix my face
with ochre, cadmium red and orange,
titanium white.
Daylight is clarified
by lemon yellow strontium,
the floorplanks scoured with ivory black.

I care for the words themselves:
alizarine, viridian, cobalt.
I turn "cerulean" over in my mouth,
curling my tongue around it;

I roll it along my teeth, surreptitiously,
like a sourball.
Our methods impede each other.
You ask me to sit still.

We rest—only to compare
our miseries
as artists, women, feminists.
The world misunderstands us.
We two misunderstand this much,
at least, about each other.

Raised consciousness requires of us
we use the using usefully,
but art demands of us
we use the using for the use itself.

A communication thin
as ink or linseed oil
has filtered, tentative, actual,
between our veins.
Translation would have been
in such a different shade or language
had both or either of us been
women but not feminists,
feminists but not artists,
artists but not women.

As it is, even our different sets of tools
recognize each other better than we do:
the rhythm of shape, the color of a vowel,
a verb's perspective,
the Manichean values of chiaroscuro,
the adjectivial danger in a composition.

The making understands itself
more than the makers do.
It has a higher consciousness,

is better organized,
and freer than you or I
shall ever be—
except in those brave moments
when we become it,
even at the price of being doomed
to blur away afterward
like the autumn light—
brightness draining from us
as from rinsed brushes;
our own selves blank, but for that visitation's jottings,
as pages in a notebook laid aside.

Meanwhile we wait for its restoration,
invoking it with all our skill—
because without it
all the organizing fails,
and I will not
quite
catch your not
quite
catching me.

FRAMES

(on the photographic art of Eva Rubinstein)

1

Each window in that deserted Rhode Island house
has white treetrunks engraved
on the panes of glass:
its only ghosts, its sole realities.

2

A woman's torso, naked in the sun,
stares from the frame through both breasts,
implacable as granite
sculpted by erosion.
Behind, beneath her, the rock itself,
her resting place, seems swollen with light,
stiff, heavy, brimming
for the suckling eye.

3

This flight of broad stone steps has waited
in shadow all day for someone to climb them,
here, in the oldest section
of an older Yugoslav city—waited,
and no footsteps echoing near.
Only now, so late, when the afternoon's last sunlight
has glanced, almost forgettingly, at this alley,
an old man, his body stooped
into a closing parenthesis, shuffles past
and, without pausing, mounts the bottom step.
Slowly, he climbs.
His breathing is labored, although the package
he carries is small—a reused paper bag
containing his supper: a wedge of bread perhaps,
some cheese, an onion. He climbs.
Now the stairs are soaked
with the sun's brief, final luminescence,

light glazing the rim of each step's shadow.
Here, just before darkness, the whole vast staircase
is glowing for him.
But he, as if he does this every day
at the same hour, continues steadily,
unhesitant, undazzled.
From level to level he rises, still stooping,
one step at a time.

4
An oval mirror
hung against flowered wallpaper
in a corner
becomes a silver lens projecting
an infinity of flowered wallpaper
to the facing wall.

5
The skin on that old woman's forehead
grains itself across her skull's burl.

6
This bed, abandoned to a mirror
in a summer room,
is empty as an altar
after the last worshiper has hurried off,
The mattress curves still
with the weight of bodiless lovers,
a cradle robbed by morning.
Yet the strewn sheets give off a radiance
that wrinkles against the walls' chipped plaster,
bounces to the ceiling, spreads
across the mirror, odalisque,
astounded at itself.
Love has been made here, or its pretense—
and if pretense, the makers alone
were ignorant of what their bodies visited

here, on this bed, abandoned to this mirror,
in this summer room.

7
Two peasant women sing
the Marbella village gossip
at one another, lyrical denunciations
through hard lips.
One gestures with her unironed laundry.
Her daughter, apart, strains
a child's bored gaze around the corner,
down what is only another street, dark
between more whitewashed walls.

8
That tree-bark, shadow-veined,
is not so dangerous with splinters
as is the nude male torso
smoothly bent, vulnerable, upon it.

9
Immaculate and orderly:
the dark wood pews stained only with age;
the aisle between their rows set
with scrubbed tiles, wide, flat,
in a diamond pattern.
Two pillars—Boaz and Jachin,
as in Solomon's temple—simply there
to bolster the ancient roof,
guard a narrow archway
toward which all the pews are facing.
No one sits in them with folded arms.
No one prays here, in this Italian synagogue
"unused since World War II."
No ark, no tabernacle, no women
leaning over the unseen balcony
to catch the unkeened words of a kaddish.
Only the light

has daavened in at the window in slow pulses
and now it wails across the wood,
the tiles, the pillars.
It settles like a tallith in the room,
subduing its folds patiently.
And from each fringe there drains
a gray illumination, trickling
toward the archway and beyond—
to the farther hall framed there,
and its distant, dark, closed door
without a knob.

10

Just now sprung furious up in bed—
her tantrum helpless, futureless as her white hair—
this skeletal old woman still can shake her fist,
still can spit out threats, showering
the nursing home with energy
malevolent from long disuse:
a Delphic majesty among the bedpans,
an Erinnye un-Eumenided,
a Norn securely sewn to bed
by crisp sheets efficiently cornered.
Only the dead, she prophesies,
have a right to patronize
the likes of her.

11

Who could abandon such a rocker,
by such a window,
even to go
and enter the view?

KINGS' GAMBIT

(for E.G. and C.S.)

They think to stand,
those famous armies of unalterable law,
guarding each their precious king
and separating queen's power
from queen's power.

Rarely, more and more often,
we are not stopped by this.
Not by the bishops burning us alive,
not by the knights' grail-gallantries
(excuses for desertion),
not even by being locked away
in castle towers, ordered to alchemize
gold from their straw.

The pawns are the great threat,
in their seeming innocence.
And the kings, of course, who can appear
powerless, needing our protection.

Rarely, more and more often,
the rules are broken
by our bold advance,
our cunning sacrifice,
our dazzling defense.
The grandest masters cannot understand.

Each time this happens,
one more fragile stone of jasper, say,

or lapis lazuli, is fixed in the mosaic
of our evolving vision.

What they forget
and what we must remember
is that each queen can move, if she chooses,
as far as she likes
in any direction.

IV

~~~~~~~~~~~~~

EASTER ISLAND

EASTER ISLAND

I Embarkation

Some have named this space where we are rooted
a place of death.
We fix them with our callous eyes
and call it, rather, a terrain of resurrection.
Love, we maintain, is more complex than theory,
is incorrect, absurd, miraculous, a contradiction,
senseless, intricate, murderous—a mystery.

Clever, but too easy, to hypothesize love
as that process by which the beloved's arbitrary face
is kindly interposed between the lover and her fear
of inattentive chaos, a universe monotone, arrythmic,
bald as the open sea.

What if, I say, a beloved face gave no such quarter
but so transluded itself into a conductor for that very sight:
eyes mandalan, primeval,
forehead opening and closing like a sea anemone
undulant for the prey startled by such loveliness,
nostrils sucking at some ether
alien from this air the lover gasps,
mouth yawing syllabic reminiscences of a lost home,
vast, empty, meaningless.

This is not pretty.
This is not *useful*, one might argue,
leaving aside outgrown romantic hypocrisies
and focusing on struggle.
We are mature now.

I am not a fool, even a holy fool.
I have wanted to settle for nothing.
I have wanted to become mature as the dolphin is mature:

a pacific complex intelligence communicating mutual mysteries
while wearing an inexhaustible wry smile;
a fish that breathes oxygen and can fly,
an underwater mammal, a dumb beast with language—
a contradiction; a witty shape at home
both in air vault and sea plunge;
monogamous with her mate for life, one with her community.
Look how she streaks her glossy understatement
like a sign, a covenant between sky and water,
an exuberant arc celebrating nothing but itself
against the gravity of blue hemming in flatter blue.

This is miraculous, but not useful.
I am not a fool nor, sadly, a mature dolphin.
I am just a woman, thirty-three years old,
trying to be useful, focusing on struggle.
Here is a man. Notice his forehead, his eyes.
He is not a fool, either.

Then there are explorers, those who would try to map us,
who want only my detailed condemnation
of this man, this struggle,
the correct impossibility of this love.
They are relieved at each clue that leads, they think,
to understanding their own pain.
It is perilous to find one's way in a city
with the guidebook to an island of volcanic rock.
We are all more intricate than that, more lost.
I must not exhort them with simplicities again,
nor permit them this: that what I risk exposing
—dead ends, short cuts, failure, exhaustive new excursions—
that these be calcified to proof
so they can claim, self-satisfied, that as they thought
the whole time, it could not be done.

This man, remember, is also not a fool,
and not, regrettably, a dolphin.
Each time they label, simplify, degrade, or chart my paleoglyphs,

impulsive, he erupts against such dogma;
their undertow of simple-mindedness
becomes a murderous riptide in his wake.
Wait. This is absurd.
If I call him murderer, it is them I fear,
their conclusions, correct lies of support that would drown him
before I could describe what else lies inland
from the shore's treachery.

What else. Year on year of sustenance, challenge, love?
Abstractions for that which resonates between us like a covenant,
unapproachable by trails of overnight analysis.
Concretions, more: molten stone thrombotic from the earth,
breathed into bedrock by our will.
This, at least: what is at stake here
is not superficial.
Support was to have been
more intricate than jargon.

Here is a man who longs for a love poem
less than my breath, inextricable from his,
its oxygen a blessing borne by trade winds.
This is deserved. That is incorrect.
Here are some others, you perhaps, most men, even some women
(not all, to be sure), who thirst for the bracing poems of hate,
uncomplicated at last as the sheer refreshing force of tropic rain.
This is deserved. That is senseless.
These are contradictions.

Because he is murderous.
Because they are murderous.
Because I murder these truths, speaking in cinders,
ash approximating what is fireflow.

I am a woman, thirty-three years old, who would be useful.
But love is more complex than theory.
The flattening rains ride on the trade winds,
they come at once, they alternate:

I suck at the wind and my face is wet.
How can I constrict this message
so it will be understood
uneasily?

II Arrival

Mariners, leaving the Netherlands where they were born,
sailed, womanless, for years
to chart the new world's waters,
sighted this island, named it a place of resurrection.
We fix them with our callous eyes
and call it, rather, a terrain of death.
We are not fools.

There are theories, none proven,
about these paleoglyphs, still undeciphered,
about these monolithic statues—
each an immensity, a brooding human face
carved from tufa, scoria, volcanic rock;
each weighing almost eight tons,
each looming near forty feet.

Some say these are the ruined deities
of a civilization more ancient than the Aztec.
Some say they are quite recent, merely
six or seven hundred years' duration,
sculpted by the Polynesians as island sentinels.
Some even say they wait, stoic as artifacts,
for the return of visitors from a distant planetary family
who carved the creatures in their image.
None can explain what leverage
could have placed such massive stones in these positions.

But love is senseless, murderous, a mystery.
All we suspect is that once, an impulsive hemorrhage of lava
for no useful reason, here, in the middle of the ocean,
bled liquid rock, layer on tier on stratum on water on air on sand

into an island, brought forth papaya and sugar cane
and tall grass in a silver tide rippling beneath trade winds,
flattened by rains, ebbing and rising above firm roots.

All we suspect is that we came to be,
crafted by some one, some culture, some unlikely distant gods,
lapicides of ourselves, perhaps, layer on year on air—
an infinitely complicated process of creation
for no reason that, so far, can be deciphered.

But we are rooted in this space,
near one another and not touching
for the analyses of tourists and cartographers.
Our presences inhale each other's adamance.
The dignity of each is original.
Notice his mouth, my forehead.
Can a cave exhale murder?
Can a sea anemone lie?
Explorers say our lavic eyes are callous,
more remote than the accessible Mayan gaze
in all its impassivity.

We do not find this so, but then
they say we were positioned
never to see each other's face,
both imaginary stares intent, instead, on the surrounding sea.
Dolphins sometimes leap there,
unstitching the horizon's seam.
Observers have no way of knowing
if we are moved by such a sight.
It is supposed we watch, these centuries,
side by side, for nothing.
This is a contradiction.

So is the exuberance I feel
to know myself erode, grateful, gradual,
scoured by the wind and porous to the rain,
my features towering downward toward the beach

in an imperceptible release from waiting
to become again the glossed density of stone,
uncarved, expressionless.

His unseen lithic face will also burl into pebbles
and sift with the shards of what were once myself,
inextricable sand at last,
none of us useful.

Meanwhile, for now, this must suffice:
that murder and resurrection are the levers of change,
that creation and complexity are one,
that miracle is contradiction.

And if, in my slow deliquescence, my face seems changed,
some alteration of my features
unaccountable to simple wind and rain,
may he perceive and may they grant
at least the possibility of a love
not easily understood,
the mystery that scorian lips can briefly wear
a dolphin smile.

V

~~~~~~~~~~~~~~~~~

THE OTHER STRAND

(for Jane Alpert)

THE TWO GRETELS

The two Gretels were exploring the forest.
Hansel was home,
sending up flares.

Sometimes one Gretel got afraid.
She said to the other Gretel,
"I think I'm afraid."
"Of course we are," Gretel replied.

Sometimes the other Gretel whispered,
with a shiver,
"You think we should turn back?"
To which her sister Gretel answered,
"We can't. We forgot the breadcrumbs."

So, they went forward
because
they simply couldn't imagine the way back.

And eventually, they found the Gingerbread House,
and the Witch, who was really, they discovered,
the Great Good Mother Goddess,
and they all lived happily ever after.

The Moral of this story is:

Those who would have the whole loaf,
let alone the House,
had better throw away their breadcrumbs.

THE PEDESTRIAN WOMAN

She stands at the intersection, waiting
to stride across in that inimitable way of hers,
shoulderbag banging against one hip, head high,
her hair promiscuous to the wind.

Or sits at the typewriter, inconspicuous
as any other woman,
writing messages to the universe
which will get her in trouble with the boss.

No past, no future, flickers like a clue
in all those chance encounters
that accumulate a life.

See her ride the subway. See her
warm the leftovers for her supper.
See her feed her dog.
And can you see what vision
fires its shape in her sleep's kiln,
what passion, irony, and wit,
what love, what courage
are disguised
in all her daily movements?

Ordinary is a word that has no meaning.

Her life is a fine piece of Japanese pottery
in the Shibui style,
so crafted that to see the cup's exterior
is to be privy only to its dull sienna clay
and to the flavored warmth with which you choose to fill it.

But drained of all your preconceptions
you may discover the bowl inside—

a high-glazed hyacinth blue
that rushes to your heart
and there remains, like an indelible message
you remember from a fortune told in tea leaves once,
like a wet jasmine flower
that you can never rinse away.

TO A WIDOW

Who am I
to dance on the grave
of the man you've lost?

Myself, locked into struggle
with one about whom
I wish many things but
very
rarely wish that he were dead.

Never mind that I recognized in you
the juggling act,
dissembling smile, explanatory shrug,
the discreet internal hemorrhage
of the spirit.

Never mind the mark he set on your life,
like a brand on a runaway slave.
Never mind, too, that you grew apart
from all his seductions
and would have utterly
changed him or utterly
left him in good time,
but were robbed even of that.

What killed him?
Murder? Execution?
Accident? Suicide?
Or did he die of a disease,
malignant masculinity,
terminal?

Or did he leap at last
into the ultimate rigidity

rather than risk a greater dying
into the health that you demanded—
his final turn of the key
in the lock of your guilt?

And who am I, who watch you now,
awed at such courage
that balances between a mourning
for your vision of what might have been
transformed,
and a determination to tear off the widow's weeds
for what remained unchanged—
who am I
to dance upon his grave?

No.
No, I should bring flowers
and stand in dumb grief
at such a tragedy:

that he could visit your life
unmoved and desperate
as a blind man in a cathedral,
peering across vast vaulted arches
at the echo-ache that whispers
of a rose-window-glory
he cannot understand.

I should tear my hair above his grave, and wail:
"Here lies proud ignorance."
I should strew lilies of the valley there,
and consecrate the earth,
if ever, for one moment, oh my sister,
you thought him worthy of your love.

SURVIVAL

We have survived
distance
as charted in the miles
stationed like markers
uniformly stretching from her street to mine;

we have survived
silence
such as may fall on us again, for years,
through which these poems will whisper
(may they serve);

we have survived
the absence or the presence
of men
in each other's lives;

we have survived
not having lain
in the arms of the other's reflection;

we have survived
not sealing off
any
possibilities;

we have survived
the rarity with which we are unable
to finish mutual sentences;

we have survived
her step, sure-footed and well-shod
hiking in the mountains,

which I, dry-mouthed with terror and embarrassment,
skidded after her in my ball-bearing sneakers;

we have survived
jails and supermarkets, our shared and apostatic
Jewishness, paychecks, shock absorbers, puppy shit,
busy signals, misplaced keys, pigments
of our imagination,
and all the other threads we trail through any life's fabric;

we have survived
even our interknotted now commitment
to us and other women,
even our love,
and certainly our fear.

And yet, this barrier.
What stands between us
she said once with a quiet laugh
against which I squinted in irrational sunlight:
what really stands between us, she said then,
is being alive.

And that, you can be sure, we will survive.

A CEREMONY

A clearing in a grove of oak,
night sounds, and water rushing
along a canyon river.
Two candles moved through the trees,
two women. The flames curved in the summer wind
like liquid leaning into gravity.

The light encircled us,
the moonrays palpable and warm.
Our pilgrimage along the dried stream-bed
completed, we stood before three giant cacti:
virgin, mother, crone—
round as massive cabbage roses
in a sacred cluster.

The roseate cactus,
seal of all my madness,
whose circle of white-tipped spines
I once had seen reach for me, stretch
for the impaling of my drawn face.

Now you said
you had never seen my lips
wear such a smile before.
Nor had I ever heard your voice like this:
sweet, high, and clear as my child's singing.
We lit the incense we had brought with us
and watched its smoke trace our calligraphy
upon a slate of air.

There is almost no one who would understand
what we were doing, and not doing, there.
There were no categories for that space.
It was simply that we had been spoken of by others

for so long, and now we spoke ourselves,
uttering a silver ring, a silver pentacle,
a cup of wine spilled carefully.
Some would have said we were not even lovers.

Look, we have left the grove.
We will grow old, and older.
One of us will die, and then the other.
The earth itself will be impaled
on sunspokes. It doesn't matter.
We have been imprinted on the protons
of energy herself,

and so stand in another atmosphere,
where an undiscovered star we will never live to see
casts shadows on a grove of succulents we cannot yet imagine.
There our interchangeable features still vibrate and blur,
each smile half of one circle,
each utterance spiraling like light
upward in shudders along the spine
as if the moon and you and I were slivers
of one mirror, gazing on herself at last.

VI

~~~~~~~~~~~~~~~~

THE NETWORK
OF THE
IMAGINARY MOTHER

THE NETWORK OF
THE IMAGINARY MOTHER

1   The Mother

"There is nothing you cannot be,"
she said crossly, "if you want to be it enough."
Momma, all her unfinished poems glued amber
on pages embrittled in notebook reliquaries;
Momma, who came a virgin to the man she loved,
who lay with him through nights when the yellow star,
his Dachau constellation, glowed again in all his dreams;
Momma, who waxed with me, the bastard daughter
he had offered to acknowledge if it were a son;
Momma, who fought for my life inside her womb
as he had fought for his outside the ovens;
who threatened to disbelieve him Jew, to call him Nazi
unless he granted me his name—and when he did,
refused it, choosing her own and mine instead
from that of Merlin's old arch-enemy,
witch-queen, sorceress.

Now she stood scrying for me whole worlds
of what no one could stop me from becoming:
art, music, science, wealth, influence, fame,
each threaded hook tugging at my child's excitement
as we fed the ducks in Bronxville Pond
and watched our bread sink upon their waters,
a propitiation to the waterlilies' soot-gray petals.
She loved Blake's etchings, then, and Kafka's tales,
the *Appassionata*, and Lao-tzu's mysteries.
And I was her miracle, her lever, her weapon,
the shuttle of her loom.
I didn't mind that until later, didn't suffocate
within it yet, but loved instead the very smell
of her terrycloth bathrobe, comforting myself

with its odor of her when she had to work late
at the lingerie counter and my aunt put me to bed
before Momma returned.

> And this is the fragrance, almost forgotten,
> that warms the deepest dreams of us all—
> even the large male children who grow
> to fear, or conquer, or imitate its power;
> even the large female children who find ourselves
> rocking each other, or men, or babies—
> we, the living totems of that rhythmic breast
> that rocked us, and which we have become,
> yet long for still.

Her power—when did I begin to sense its origins?
When did I embrace my disgust
at this gross world, her fat body, my own flesh?
Was it there with the first contraction,
when my outraged head thudded stubborn
against her pelvis, turning itself aside
again, again, in my refusal to leave her?
—or when, after being dragged alive
into a sick yellow dawn by double forceps,
this matter and energy of me, unreconciled,
met in the initial skirmish of a battle to the death:
convulsions jerking the puppet baby
every four hours for the first two days?
By the age of ten I felt stayed in the corset of my ribs,
basted to my spine, sausaged into my skin.
A few years after, I would write about Icarus:
> "The shed husk lies upon the ground
> and one is free."
Still later, I read Teilhard de Chardin
and wept with lust for deliverance into spirit,
light, soul, intellect.
This blood was not of my making.
These breasts were not of my willing.
There is nothing you cannot be if you want it enough.

She had lied more than once.

I felt her watch me with a superfluity of eyes,
reach for me with eight arms,
spidery as an Eastern goddess.
She seemed to sit at the center of my life,
secreting my future, dividing herself
into two half-bodies, one of which was meant for me.
I fought her architecture, her manipulations,
calling her three-faced, thinking her common
though organic, and certainly original.

And all these cycles later, all the scenes
and silent intervals and tears, what is left between us?
That blood was my own, those breasts were all I knew.
They hang empty now; all her pulp sags jaundiced, flaccid,
rippling from her palsied limbs.
What is intolerable here
is the voice of a three-year-old child in me
who cries that with this death the world is ending:
Age Unlimited, the wreckers, are tearing down
my first home.
Paid by the hour, they take their time.

Where Blake and Lao-tzu once mused,
unreformed rabbis rave, now, in her brain's asylum.
Doctors incise, lawyers unravel
her frenzied weaving of lawsuits, wills, stock-market deals.
She disowns all her transformations.
She wants to make a killing before she dies.

How can she recognize my real inheritance—
that I became an heiress long ago of her indifference
to the celebration of her own body
or another woman's, or a man's
—this, her means of enduring;
the lesson passed to me, the knot
untangled still by thirty years of patience,

by three decades of courage still uncut.
Not that this is all she gave me,
although the matriheritage left her impoverished.
She shuffles at each curb, shifting her feet
while her forehead breaks out in rhinestones of sweat:
she cannot estimate how deep the step is.
Her whole body tremors with Parkinson's
lascivious dybbuk, as if her torso
were a giant heart, pumping its spasms
along attendant arteries, her puppet limbs.
She is too strong to die of this, though—
a mere degenerative disease.

She will be murdered by attack
when one day quite soon now
a small, arteriosclerotic organ
the size of her clenched fist,
unnourished by the living current beating
hopeless in blocked passageways,
unable to release
all that congested, shameless, scarlet love
for its own body:
when one day this heart—her actual heart—implodes.
Meanwhile, she is afraid to read my poems, that best of me
I offer her—afraid she will not understand them
or afraid she will.
She waits alone with still more Yahrzeit candles each Yom Kippur,
alone, and I intransigent in my own fierce survival,
knowing at last her way is not my way.

But there must be some honor even in survival.
So when she fell and lay six hours unable to reach the phone,
and then was sped to the hospital where we—yes, They and I—
fought for weeks to break her will in order to save her life,
and when she returned, a barren invalid, to her apartment's clutter,
the lure of my blood was there before me.
Helpless, I waded back upstream to where I had been born
to give her birth this time—brutal as she, after all,

merciless, bullying the medication into her decrescent body,
learning at last and bitterly and utterly:
The life comes first. There is no spirit without the form.

> And this is the knowledge, almost remembered,
> that chills the deepest nightmares of us all—
> the grown male children who fear the wheel
> is turned by Kali's dancing; the grown female
> children who lose ourselves, complacent,
> to only one of the Three Aspects: Virgin, Mother, Crone,
> and then deny the numinous presence of the other Two
> in any woman, in terror of what we are becoming,
> yet long for still.

Vile. This is vile. This is the Mystery
from which my inmost flesh-revulsion springs.
This loathing, now, to kneel between these massive thighs
squatting in pain; to bear this bedpan like a chalice
for the dregs of her life's untold hagiography;
to lie such set responses of encouragement and comfort.
Here is the truth I flee from in my own body—
the cosmic wit of each cell's purulescence:
this stench of death and urine, this bulging pubes
flecked with matted hair.
Here are your gates of eternity, your pit, your trapdoor,
your fissure in the earth before which the priestess sways.
Here is the lair of tabu, the grove of ritual.
Here I was born.

I am up to my elbows in filth,
inescapably undead.
There is no cleansing from this.
There is only rage, and the instinct older than love
that thrusts my arms in deeper,
grasping the life that is her, is myself,
the spirit raining pus for iridescence,
the infection of being alive
which I shall never again disclaim.

Momma, I will be with you when you die.

Repeat the syllables
until the lesson is drummed along the arteries:
Margaret Jones, midwife, hanged 1648.
Joan Peterson, veterinarian, hanged 1652.
Isobel Insch Taylor, herbalist, burned 1618.
Mother Lakeland, healer, burned 1645.

What have they done to you?

2   The Consort

Say what you will, there is this man.
Correct or incorrect, father-figure, faggot, fool,
or any other pat conclusion you assume be damned.
There is this man.
I who hate the class of men have loved this man
for almost half my life. Nothing,
not even him, will stop me now.
Certain things are understood between us.

Yes, I was seventeen, and suicidal, and a poet.
Yes, he was ten years older, suicidal, and a poet.
(We may be suicidal but we're hardly self-destructive.)
It was the bond of poetry no one could comprehend:
that what his mind contained appeared to me
as an interior castle, its crystal terraced
radiant through the body I desired and feared.
The litanies of struggle, of despair, I've intoned elsewhere
and doubtless will again: once to have said such things
was thought unspeakable.
Unfashionable, now, to sing:
radiant, you see, spirit in matter,
pulsant with energy, the word made flesh.

Say what you will, I was not wrong.

This is now the thirteenth year
since I came virgin to him, to the one man
I have loved, since I first lay with him
through nights when all his lovers
haunted our dream-streets, mocking their maleness and his;
averting their eyes from me, his transgression,
his sin—my body the glowing sign
of his desertion from their numbers.
This is the thirteenth year
since that cheap votive candle stuttered its light
on the bedsheet where my ritual blood
pooled like wax for the signet of our embrace.

See, these are the poems we tore from one another,
these are the scars.
The stitches have been absorbed.
At first I knew only his power.
At first he set his seal upon me.
At first he could not have known my power
or understood the misuse of his own.
At first we were drawn solely by what we would become.

But this is the thirteenth year,
and we are drawn by what we have always been,
always, before breath, poems, dreams
could inhabit us.
Now is my seal set upon him,
as it was in the beginning
when we foamed up from my imagination, infinite,
and exploded into our innumerable selves.
Here is your matter and energy,
your electrons and protons.
Here is my ecstatic whim, primordial,
the DNA pattern purled light-speed from my needles;
the immaculate violent ordure of this cauldron
from which all entities crawl—

the insouciant earthworm, the maga clam
who divides herself,
experiments with making that part
of her macro-organismic possibility
male,
the complement, the consort,
the curious delightful novelty of him.

He approaches his tryst, the anthropodiacal lover:
 Eager to please, he proudly tiptoes, eight-legged,
   toward me on the surface of the waters.
   He offers food.
   If I accept the gift, his courtship may begin.
 Eager to amuse, he jumps in his excitement,
   waving gaudy striped legs, hopping in self-congratulation
   at having found me.
 Eager to arouse, he sidles in a cunning rhythm
   near where I may observe him; he pantomimes
   how he would wrap me loosely
   in a special mating canopy of silk.
Spinning, I cast down my dragline for his ascent.
I disown none of my transformations.

And ever since,
leisurely, through all the thirteen orphic eternities,
we have been quickening toward each other
in this saraband:
 Exchanging lanquidities with our lama eyes;
 Keening a seaweed counterpoint in our great blue whale voices
   across the ocean's amphitheaters;
 He, his electric-maned head suddenly lifted, nostrils flaring
   to catch the lioness scent of me whole deserts distant;
 I centripetaling down my ladder of air, drawn by the beacon-fire
   his feathers spread for me in a strutting audition—
   such phosphorescent greens and violets;
 Salt mellow on our tongues from tasting each others' skin and tears.
Ever since, a floating through sameness and difference,
poems like sparks of laughter

struck from the flint of our diversionary griefs.
This is possible.
I have said so.

He has feared I divide myself, divide him:
mind and body, spirit and flesh, the cosmic and the daily.
As if I could settle for nothing.
I say to him, yes, there are certain reasons
I have done this—among them, choicelessness;
as if the center of my life were knotted up
into a hub of memory, itself unspeakable,
from which is spoken all that moves me.
I say to him that such a clot will never be dissolved
except along paths radiating order
which only *then* can be ignored—as each spoke
must be balanced with precision on a wheel
in preparation merely to blur invisible
once the wheel spins.
The means and goal must justify each other.
For how many millennia must the river sculpt the canyon?
How opaque must the winter sleep become
before the Northern Lights will visit the eye?
I say to him:
Why have I called you "Mother" in my dreams?

> And this is the question, almost unwhispered,
> that wakens the riddled nights of us all—
> the grown male children who dare not yet answer
> what the grown female children yet dare not ask:
> where is the reason for loving? who risked inventing it?
> how large must we grow before giving birth to each other,
> a labor we fear to begin each dawn,
> yet long for still.

I affirm all of my transformations.

For this is the thirteenth year
and I am come into my power.

I say to him:
There is a place beyond our struggle
where I will take us—
beyond the archetypal, the animal,
even the human,
beyond all we have been so far.
It will exist, see, I am creating it now.
You are utterly given over unto me.
And I will make of you the beloved,
I will call sacred antlers up from your brow
and place pipes against your lips.
Your haunches are mine, your sly buttocks,
your body disarrayed of all but my arms' garlands,
your brain encelled with my brain, double lotus.
Before your Osirian trance will I unveil myself.
You shall be again the luminous bridegroom
all my suffering foresaw—
upon whose groin I placed my palm
to consecrate the light that streamed
from all your prophecies.

We shall never be finished.
I name you
husbandman.
I say:
There is this man.
I claim him.
Blessed be, it is he I have chosen.

> *Repeat the syllables*
> *until the lesson is pumped through the heart:*
> *Nicriven, accused of lasciviousness, burned 1569.*
> *Barbara Gobel, described by her jailors*
> *as "the fairest maid in Wurzburg,"*
> *burned 1629, age nineteen.*
> *Frau Peller, raped by Inquisition torturers*
> *because her sister refused*
> *the witch-judge Franz Buirman, 1631.*

Maria Walburga Rung, tried at a secular court
in Mannheim as a witch,
released as "merely a prostitute,"
accused again by the episcopal court
at Eichstadt, tortured into confession,
and then burned alive, 1723, age twenty-two.

What have they done to me?

3   The Sister

There are these women's faces, a montage
of features so like my own, though darker or older
or thinner or sweeter. They have names each,
and unique identical secrets. Lady of the Sorrows.
Lady of the Plants. Lady of the Scales.
These are my people.
The lattice of my spine shudders with such a weight.

There are these women's faces, various
as dewprints sequined across my life's web,
every grain reflecting a different dawn.
The interlace of all my years shudders with such a weight
until each pod of moisture bursts,
flooding toward the center—
that hub of memory, itself unspeakable,
from which is spoken all that moves us.

There is this woman's face,
she for whom I have spun out of myself
whole networks of survival.
"Each with the one weapon the other most needed
at that moment."
Who could have dreamt that the weapons
simply would be ourselves,

placed each in the other's keeping?
The love that, once, did not dare speak its name
may lie in silence yet for reasons other
than even you and I assume—life and death reasons
beyond a mere surviving.

Perhaps if these six years that lie behind us
had not also lain between us,
perhaps if we had not met one spring equinox too late,
perhaps I might have sung then
what since I have been forced to whisper
in too many bad translations, a luxury
of plain details, such as:
—My dear, that birthmark high on your right cheek
actually is a virus, the devil's stamp
they would have called it once, a life form improbable
as an albino olive blithely afloat
in a cup of its own greengold Nile oil.
Your eyelids are Mycenean; they cradle
the fertile crescents of your eyes—
perhaps.

Instead, the ancient tragedy of women closed around us,
our version identical with every other, unique
only in minute details of Eleusinian translation
reenacted, even as my arms reached to close round you
—the daughter I thought I'd found,
the mother I thought I'd lost,
Oh Demeter, oh Kore—
then something rose and walked again in me
and would not let me rest until
I could stand scrying for you worlds
of what no one could stop you from becoming,
until you were my miracle, my lever, the shuttle
of my loom, you not even minding that,
not suffocating in it, yet.

When did you begin to sense my power?

Your own was so different, so indifferent,
alive with reckless sensuality
to answer all my sentience.
You would freeze me on camping trips,
contort me into yoga knots,
melt me in hot-springs baths,
hammering like a metronome against my fugue
your signature: the physical.
And all the while my wondering
if you were part of this plot that would embody me.

If so, then move by move, and all but motionless,
I still have beaten you at chess, by god.
I have wrenched your brain into places
you fancied I might.
I have mourned with you
and I have densified myself into a magnet
strong as you always demanded it to be,
stronger than you intended to resist.
When the holy sea-mammal gives birth
there is another dolphin, the dolphin-midwife
they call her, to attend and to assist the labor.
So I tracked you, relentless,
to where you patiently fled my arrival.

Our peril was more complicated
even than you and I assumed,
though cowards will see in our love
their own lovelessness, yet remain ignorant
of what we know: to be afraid can be a moral act.

We thought ourselves such careful weavers.
We never meant to choose our pattern
from the marble of that Aegean figure:
the goddess daughter statued on the goddess mother's head—
yet history let no other model stand for us
unbroken or reclaimed: even those two women
exchanging gifts on the Pharsalian stele,

a balance of sisters who appear equals of each other
and of the task as well—these two are also
Demeter and Kore.

And so I saw myself begin to watch you
with a superfluity of eyes,
felt you reach for me as with eight arms,
until I came to sit at the center of your life,
secreting your future, dividing myself
into two half-bodies, one of which was meant for you.
At times you fought my architecture, my manipulations.
At other times you cried without me that the world was ending.
There is nothing you cannot be if you want it enough, I said.

      And this is the prophecy, almost ignored,
      that lies like a truth beneath our desiring to will
      our will to desire: the large male children
      who would secretly conquer themselves in each other;
      the grown female children who would rather not conquer
      at all, even those selves we flee in disgust from,
      yet long for still.

Now must your seal be set upon yourself.
Another 'must'? Another.
To nurture what we have delivered,
you must spin networks of survival
all of your own imagining.
Then, then it can be said
that you are beautiful to me
as the rare flower of a roseate cactus,
your loveliness wild as a blizzard of mountain snow,
your smile lazy and then sudden as the dance of a young lizard.

Now, like a sybil, I can see
that where you walk, a new Persephone blinking in the light,
tendrils verdant with possibilities
tremble awake, there, in your footprints.
One bears an orb of tiny flowers,

a circlet of lace pale as the new moon's pledge,
a sable star at its heart,
sealing the cancellation of all debts between us—

that this release might teach us both
how all my mother posturing and all your daughter mime
was played out after all by siblings, the grown female children
of an older One whose quick sagacity
has watched us with more than a single pair of eyes:
air-breathing arachnid, She whose body
is divided into two equal and balanced parts,
whose hidden spinnerets secrete a liquid
that the air hardens into silk
as useful for wrapping eggs as luring enemies,
for knitting gossamer balloons from which to swing while riding
the currents of summer to her chosen destination—
and oh, for wreathing the symmetry of a mandala,
this other network, original, organic
as a common orb-web, its quatro-corners
anchored to fire, water, earth, and air,
radiant from the hub whose spokes unspeakably
still move us.

No longer Demeter in such a different dawn, Persephone,
I feel my gaze endewed with prisms
through which I watch that hub, those spokes,
shiver, then slowly pivot, then spin free,
blurring into its revolution
The World Disc, The Great Round,
The Silver Wheel of Transformation,
within which your own life must hurtle—
one brief arc deathless as a single head
of Queen Anne's lace,
plucked from my root self involuntary as a poppy,
and lightly twirled between the palms—
a token of welcome and farewell,
a seal,
a small gift

from one woman
to another.

> Repeat the syllables
> before the lesson hemorrhages through the brain:
> Margaret Barclay, crushed to death with stones, 1618.
> Mary Midgely, beaten to death, 1646.
> Peronette, seated on a hot iron as torture
>   and then burned alive, 1462.
> Sister Maria Renata Sanger, sub-prioress
>   of the Premonstratensian Convent of Unter-Zell,
>   accused of being a lesbian;
>   the document certifying her torture
>   is inscribed with the seal of the Jesuits,
>   and the words Ad Majorem Dei Gloriam—
>   To the Greater Glory of God.

> What have they done to us?

4 The Child

Hush.
This is utterly simple.
Before you,
I did not know what it meant to love.
I did not know it was this:

> Your outraged head
> thudding stubborn against my pelvis,
> turning itself aside again, again,
> in your refusal to leave me.

> The absolutism of your eyelids,
> lilac-veined transparencies that swell
> in rhythm to the rolling of your dream.

The authority of your mouth;
its gravity, tongue-frail,
drawing up the tide from my lunar nipples.

The visitation of that laugh
you abandon me to, unasked for, sudden,
miraculous as an underground spring
unlocking the Februaries of my life.

The summer-nap smell of your body,
the grace with which you stretch on wakening, animal,
the vulnerability of your baby penis, a rosehip
blooming shameless under my all unthreatened kiss.

This blood is my own, of my own making.
Flesh of my flesh. These breasts were all you knew.
Before this, I did not understand
the luxury of skin, its velvet imperative.
You have taught me
the most ancient of pleasures.

In awe of this
have we been celebrated from the first:
the Hittite lion-mother, brazen above her child;
the Isis, hammered in copper, cupping her left breast
toward where you lean up from her lap;
the pre-Colombian effigy vessels where I smile
at your marsupial grasp;
the Yoruban wood-spools; the Celtic icons, stone-hewn;
the prehistoric bronze Sardinian pietà;
the scaraboid seal, Ionian, on which I whelp you;
the Aztec codex of the goddess Tlazolteotl;
the fifteenth-century "Vierge Ouvrante"—that virgin
whose enthroned self opens as two doors, disclosing
the world, safe, sleeping, on her knees.

And this is the reason, always denied,
that throbs like an uncut cord through the warp

of our fantasies: the large male children
who adopt each other in defiance;
the grown female children who reject the mothers
we once were—before they became the only selves
we were permitted to become,
yet long for still.

I disown
none
of my transformations.

Little heart, little heart,
you have sung in me like the spiral alder-bud.
You, who gave birth to this mother
comprehend—for how much longer?—my mysteries.
Son of my cellular reincarnation, you alone know
the words that awaken me when I play dead
in our game. You alone wave
at the wisp through which I see you.
You understand. You whisper,
"Listen—life is really going on, right now,
around us. Do you see it? Sometimes I lose it
but if I sit still and listen, it comes back,
and then I think, How funny, this is what being alive is.
Do you know?"
I have uttered you wisely.

Still, I have grieved before the time, in preparation
for my dolor, at how you will become
a grown male child, tempted by false gods.
I have been *Pisaura mirabilis*, the nursery-web spider
who carries her egg's bulk in aching jaws,
who wraps it in a weft of love,
who guards its hatching.
You have clung to me like a spiderling
to the back of the *Lycosa lenta*; Wolf-spider mother,
I have waited, whenever you fell off,
for you to scramble on again before proceeding.

But you have come five-fold years
and what I know now is nothing
can abduct you fully from the land where you were born.
I am come into my power, oh littlest love,
fruit of my flowering. I have seen you,
who feared the spinner less than her hoop's fragility
—fabric of nightmares—hold your breath at the rush of beauty
on a country dawn when we beheld her dew-glazed gauze corona.
You reached past fear, through reverence, to touch—
anointing your fingertips,
anointing all my August droughts.
And I have seen you, crowned by ivy leaves,
dance naked in a candlelit circle of stones,
your laughter offered to me like a bell cluster,
like the fat purple grapes you pelt me with,
your milk-teeth seducing my ear with nibbles.

Wars have been made against me, empires built
with the dolmen of my bones, ships have pocked
the egg of my covenant where it gleams
on their benighted path.
But there is no erasing this:
the central memory of what we are
to one another, the grove of ritual.
I have set my seal upon you.

I say:
you shall be a child of the mother
as of old, and your face will not be turned from me.
Then shall the bosom of the earth open and feed you,
rock you, safe, sleeping, on her lap.
No more will your stomachs bulge tumorous with hunger,
my children; no more will you be gaily tossed
on the soldiers' bayonet-points; no more will you scream
at the iron roar of death in the heavens;
no more will you stare through the miniature convulsions
of your newborn heroin addiction.
You shall be disinherited of all these legacies.

And in their place,
and in your footprints,
tendrils green with possibility will tremble
awake.

This you have taught me—what it is to love.
Your unmodern wisdom thudding against my pelvis,
refusing to leave me.
How can I not celebrate
this body,
your first home?

I did not know
how simple this secret would be.
How utterly simple.
Hush.

> Repeat the syllables
> before the lesson perforates the uterus:
> Anna Rausch, burned 1628, twelve years old.
> Sybille Lutz, burned 1628, eleven years old.
> Emerzianne Pichler, tortured and burned together
>   with her two young children, 1679.
> Agnes Wobster, drowned while her small son was forced
>   to watch her trial by water, 1567.
> Annabelle Stuart, burned alive, 1678,
>   fourteen years old.
> Veronica Zerritsch, compelled to dance
>   in the warm ashes of her executed mother,
>   then burned alive herself, 1754,
>   thirteen years old.
> Frau Dumler, boiled to death in hot oil
>   while pregnant, 1630.

> What have they done?

5   The Self

Each unblinking eyelet linked now
to another in the shuttles of the loom.
"Thin rainbow-colored nets, like cobwebs,
all over my skin."
I affirm
all
of my transformations:

> An autumnal mother, treading the way of life
>   past all her trials, yearns toward her Albion,
>   leperous-white as waterlilies.
> Returning to herself, a daughter who reflects
>   a different dawn emerges, reckless as the weeds
>   that array her vernal equinox.
> The chosen man, given over at last, discards his shroud
>   for love's reweaving, initiate to what
>   the ecstatic Widow male has always known, the secret
>   of the young king at winter solstice—
> And so is born again, shameless, laughing,
>   to reach past fear, through reverence, to touch
>   what it is like, this being alive.

These are my people.

They are of my willing, of my own making.
I have invented them no less than I create myself,
thought imagining shape, uttering existence.
To understand this universe I fabricate
—my cosmic joke, embodied plot—
I am become the Spinner, giving out of myself
myself the Egg,
taking into myself
myself the Prey.

Witch-queen, sorceress,
I must live within this body, my final home—
here to decode each runic fingerprint,

to trust the assurance of each hair's whitening,
to recognize the clue left by each stretch-mark.
My taste is salty, my smell ammonial.
My knuckles can crack like willow-bark
and hairblades cover my hide
stubborn as fine grass.
My nails are crisp as relics
and every crevice—armpits, crotch,
toe-valleys, ears, mouth, nostrils, eyes—exudes
mucous or sweat for iridescence.
Oh let me learn that I am beautiful to me,
innocent as the spider—
beyond judgment, disgust, beyond perfection—
reconciled with her tufted claw,
with the matted topaz of my labia.
Let me sit at the center of myself
and see with all my eyes,
speak with both my mouths,
feel with all my setae,
know my own sharp pleasure,
learning at last and blessedly and utterly:
The life comes first. There is no spirit without the form.

Drawn from the first by what I would become,
I did not know how simple this secret could be.
The carapace is split,
the shed skin lies upon the ground.
I must devour the exoskeleton of my old shapes,
wasting no part, free only then
to radiate whatever I conceive,
to exclaim the strongest natural fiber known
into such art, such architecture
as can house a world made sacred by my building.
Sheet method, funnel, and orb,
each thread of the well-named Ariadna
unreels its lesson:

The Triangle web, three-faced as my aspects;

the filmy Dome web, a model firmament;
the domesticity of the Bowl-and-Doily web;
the droll zig-zag of the Filistata;
the Hammock pattern's indolence;
the Coras web, with healing power for welts and fever;
the Trapdoor web, shield of the White Lady from the desert;
the Arabesca, the Dictyna;
the vaporous Platform web;
the Umbrella's unfolding tension;
the esoteric Pyramid design;
the Purse web, tubed and tightly wattled;
the Bubble web, patience iterated underwater,
a crystal castle of air.

Here is discipline, imagination, variation.
Here are your paragons, my avatars.

I am learning.
The cord is wrapped around my throat.
I am learning.
The passageway is cramped and blind
I am learning
though Kali dances through it, past
where Demeter still seeks Persephone,
where Isis searches for the fragments of Osiris,
where I wade upstream through a living current
which seizes me and drowns me into life,
pumping, pumping, as from a giant heart
whose roar I have called Mother in my dreams.

> *What do you remember?*
> *What is it that you long for still?*

Oh let me hear you hear
me speak oh
speak to
me oh let me

Repeat the syllables
each cell has unforgotten:
There was the Word before their word.
The Silence came.
The Name was changed.

What have they done to themselves?

What have they dared,
sucking at man's wounds for wine,
celebrating his flesh as food?
Whose thirst has been slaked by his vampire liquor,
whose hunger answered by his ghostly bread?

Who have they dared to hang on that spine instead
and then deny, across millennia?
Whose is the only body which incarnates creation
everlasting?

As it was in the beginning,
   I say:
   Here is your sacrament—

         Take. Eat. This is my body,
         this real milk, thin, sweet, bluish,
         which I give for the life of the world.
         Like sap to spring it rises
         even before the first faint cry is heard,
         an honest nourishment
         alone able to sustain you.

   I say:
   Here is your eternal testament—

         This cup, this chalice, this primordial cauldron
         of real menstrual blood
         the color of clay warm with promise,
         rhythmic, cyclical, fit for lining the uterus

and shed for many,
for the remission of living.

Here is your bread of life.
Here is the blood by which you live in me.

The World Disc, The Great Round,
The Wheel of Transformation.
Two solstices, summer and winter.
Two equinoxes, spring and fall.
One day to stand outside the year, unutterable.
Thirteen-fold is my lunar calendar,
Five-fold my mysteries, my kiss,
Three-fold my face.

And this is the secret, once unquestioned,
sought in the oldest trances of us all:
the large male children forced into exile
from their pelvic cradle, wailing, refusing to leave;
the grown female children, knotting together the skein
of generations, each loop in the coil a way back
to that heart of memory we cannot escape,
yet long for still.

No more need you dream this, my children,
in remembrance of me.
There is a place beyond your struggle
where I will take us.
It will exist, see, I am creating it now.
I have said so.

Blessed be my brain
that I may conceive of my own power.
Blessed be my breast
that I may give sustenance to those I love.
Blessed be my womb
that I may create what I choose to create.
Blessed be my knees

        that I may bend so as not to break.
    Blessed be my feet
            that I may walk in the path of my highest will.

Now is the seal of my vision
set upon my flesh.

You call me by a thousand names, uttering yourselves.

        Earthquake I answer you, flood and volcano flow—
                the Warning.
                This to remind you that I am the Old One
                who holds the Key, the Crone to whom all things return.

        Lotus I answer you, lily, corn-poppy, centripetal rose—
                the Choice.
                This to remind you that I am the Mother
                who unravels from herself the net sustaining you.

        Moon I answer you, my gibbous eye, the regenerating carapace,
                the Milky Way—
                the Possibility.
                This to remind you that I am the Virgin
                born only now, new, capable of all invention.

I have been with you from the beginning,
utterly simple.
I will be with you when you die,
say what you will.
We shall never be finished.
This is possible,
a small gift, hush.

There is nothing I have not been,
and I am come into my power.

There is nothing I cannot be.

VII

~~~~~~~~~~~~

NORNS

THE DANCE OF THE SEVEN VEILS

This, the first veil, the scarlet
for my mother and all her sisters
who recognize the blood-rite, who know
which revelations could dismember
the mosaic of this world
but fear the cost, who love me
but go veiled.
To them I sacrifice the first.
See where it pulses, a forbidden standard
raised rebelliously above a conquered city.

This, the second veil, the violet,
for the king and all his brothers
who offer half their empires in return
for my possession, ignorant that I require
in its entirety what has always been my own.
To them I fling the second.
See where it flies, like royal spittle,
my laughter answering their lust.

This, the third veil, the cerulean,
for all the stillborn hopes arterial
along my limbs, blue as the veins of my children
never now to be conceived,
blue as the shadows of hunger moulding the faces
of those already living in hope of bread
outside the gates of every palace.
To these I entrust the third,
See where it ripples like a salty mist
over the sea's grief.

This, the fourth veil, the emerald,
for the false prophet and all his prisoners
of envy, matricidal messiahs

who turn in disgust from the female,
rutting for death instead, for martyrdom
as hosted by their jealous god.
For them I discard the fourth.
See where it billows like indifferent grass,
an obstinate renewing above the grave.

This, the fifth veil, the saffron,
for the soldier and all his followers,
cowards who will slay me pretending they obey orders
other than their own, but desperate themselves
to cover my golden holy nakedness with their spiked shields
before such splendor dazzles, delivers, and unmans them.
To my assassins I bequeath the fifth.
See where it flickers to their feet and lies,
their only spoil.

This, the sixth veil, the white,
for myself, intended for a crown
who chose instead this craft:
each leap a calculation practiced
to exact, as if by effortless abandon,
the transcendent selves of those who witness it,
like the lunar dancer drawing after her her tides.
Yet no audience, at the last, moves either of us:
ourself the purpose, price, and prize.
To me, the sixth, the silver veil, I dedicate.
See where it floats, my spirit
whirling with love about my flesh.

This, the seventh veil, transparent,
for the dance itself.
Unspeakable
as the letters of my stolen name,
without color, as the air glows, palpable.
Only this presence, like a length of space,
a skin sloughed, a rendered breath.
To the dance alone the seventh veil is cast.

See where it shimmers,
a membrane shuddering open—
spent, vacant now,
an afterbirth.

THE SPIDER WOMAN

What pose would draw you toward me,
what mask hold you here?
The Lady who grants you her hem to kiss?
The Child whose laughter wakes your youth?
The Maiden who trembles, chaste with longing?
Or The Spider Woman, who waits and spins
nerves of desire around your brain,
and knows us best, and usually wins?

> Whichever face I choose to hide
> her skull manipulates, not mine.
> She smoothes me like a subtle thread.
> I feel her live along my line.

You can flay the gown from The Lady's back,
you can maim The Child to a coy grotesque,
you can rape The Maiden into chastity.
But though you set your poems of love
like iridescent pearlblue flies
across The Spider Woman's silk,
she never was and will not be deceived.

> Yet I must hack away each night
> strands I secrete more easily each day,
> or I will be ensnared, myself, too tight
> to act as if I were your prey.

Grown mad, but with a spider's grace,
The Lady crawls to smother The Child
whose rasping laughter wakens The Maiden
to visions of a jealous lover
whose eight legs twine about her hips.
I shine here naked, free of my disguises.
I hang in the web so that you may see

not only grief at your temptation,
but rage that expands me to ten times your size;
not only hunger from many lives of fasting,
but this core of endurance to will you toward me.

Step lightly now, my love, approach me if you dare.
How you are drawn by the red flower of my belly!
One move, my love, without the greatest care—
and you become to me

an aftertaste, a poem, a pearlblue fly.

THE MERMAID

(a lullaby, for Blake)

Once there was a mermaid
who lived in the sea.
She was as happy
as a mermaid can be,
as happy as you and me.

One day a fisherman came by
and caught her in his net.
He dragged her back to land
and
there she sat.

He laughed at her and said that he
a wealthy man would be,
for people they would pay to watch
a mermaid from the sea.

He laughed at her and then he turned
and went a little way;
wrapping his cloak about himself,
down on the sand he lay.

The sun went down, the moon came up
over the silver beach.
The mermaid strained to touch the tide
ebbing beyond her reach.

The fisherman slept.
The mermaid wept.

She called out to her Mother Sea
and to her sister fish.
She cried to them, "Come rescue me,
that is my only wish."

The foam heard her, the fish heard her,
the creatures of the sea:
dolphin and whales, shrimp, squid, clams, crabs,
and sea anemone.

The waves and creatures heard her cry;
they swept onto the land.
They drowned the fisherman where he lay
sleeping on the sand.
He never saw a richer day.

The creatures came and gnawed the net
and set their sister free.
Then mermaid, waves, and fish were swept
back to their Mother Sea.

The mermaid lives within the waves,
happy as she can be,
happy as you and me.
And if you chance to see her there,
smile and go away,

for great the Wrath and wild the Rage
on any who would dare
to tear
a mermaid from her Mother Sea,
or you
from me.

THE BEGGAR WOMAN

Fact scums a mirage upon my retina,
an afterimage, a negative apparition.

    Some nights I sit cross-legged in the driveway,
    burnoose-wrapped, a live pyramid.

As if this ice-cube's transpiration behind glass were real.
As if that beetle could be hesitating on the wall.

    Some nights the driver runs me over
    or worse, leaves gravel in the cup instead of coins.

As if I could still choose.
Dawn after city dawn I tense horizontal as spent rain.

    Some nights the child waits with me, ribs stretching
    its gourd-hollow skin, a silent drum on my lap.

As if this hunger could be fed.
As if your love could fill me.

    Some nights the Angel of Death rides by, ignoring us,
    reading the Book of Life inside his limousine's black temple.

As if my own hand were not fused to the hilt of this dagger.
As if the blade were not serrated by my will.

    Some nights I think they leave, circle, and return
    only to be sure I think they do.

As if I could still hesitate.
As if that ice of me could melt to rain.

Some night the wheels will slow, the door will open,
if they can be convinced that I am harmless.

As if I could not steel my life inward toward the act,
the way stones poise before they avalanche on one veiled head.

LA DOÑA SEBASTIANA

This face and body, carved from a tree,
resemble the real me.

Wood skeleton, not bone.
Wood skull, not calcium.
Sap-seep, not marrow or gluey blood.
See the grain in her forehead,
the understated knotholes of her temples.

La Doña Sebastiana,
Lady of Arrows,
what village genius whittled your death-size perfection,
moderating your radical nakedness
with only a cloak of unbleached linen,
your bald extremism with hair of plaited straw?
You smile no answer.

They build you every year
for Holy Week, for the Procession
of Penitentés
in the older villages of Mexico and Peru.
They carve you a small oak cart, as well,
in which you are reverently drawn
through the streets, silent with people,
through the world.

They heap the cart with flowers
extravagant as skin.
But the economical angle of your arm
bears only wheat sheaves.
You are not fooled.

None may reach out to touch you
but the legend tells

that each Procession your sheaf will brush one
—only one—
in the waiting crowd.
And that one will never fear again,
so blessed by the grazing of the Lady of Death.
What more is there to fear?

Two days later, they burn
the cart, the wheat, the dried flowers,
the planed geometry of you,
to celebrate the resurrection of their christ.
They have done this for three thousand years,
have built you, borne you, burned you
when Bethlehem was not yet settled.
They no longer know why.

But I know why, La Doña Sebastiana,
Woman of Wood and Wheat,
Lady of Death.

I first heard your cartwheels'
cobbled rhythm
when I was five years old,
waiting in bed one night.

As a young girl,
I glimpsed your silhouette flash near
in glances between sleep and waking.
I have felt alien here
a long time.

And lately, I have breathed their rotting flowers
as penance,
have felt my hair-ends split like straw.

Doña Sebastiana,
Mother of Trees and Grain,
Mother of Death,

I have been an orphan now for enough seasons
where you left me, a foundling
on this doorstep.
I want my heritage.

I want my head plucking silence
like a pic on the strings of your ribs.
I want my fingers rising from the dirt
as wheat.
I am alien, alien here.

But I am patient, disciplined
as a village artisan.
I know better than to reach for you,
a vulgar grasp at what will come to me.
I am your daughter.

For you have brushed me, Lady,
claimed me for your own
as lightly as a spear of wheat
ruptures the air,
as irreversible.

There is still the end of the Procession,
and the dismantling, and the fire.
But I, your solitary child, at least am where
I know now
they can never save me.

VIII

~~~~~~~~~~~~~~~~~

VOICES
FROM SIX TAPESTRIES

(for Kenneth Pitchford)

THE CHOOSING OF THE JEWELS
The Weavers Speak

HEARING
The Handmaiden Speaks

SMELL
The Lion Speaks

TASTE
The Monkey Speaks

TOUCH
The Unicorn Speaks

SIGHT
The Lady Speaks

In the Musée de Cluny in Paris hangs a set of six tapestries: *La Dame à la Licorne* (*The Lady with the Unicorn*). Five of the tapestries have as their themes the senses; the sixth has been called "The Choosing of the Jewels"—we are not certain in which order they were intended to be displayed. All six date from the fifteenth century (approximately) and were evidently woven in high-warp technique of wool and silk, about fifteen warp threads to the inch. Opinion differs on the place of origin; some scholars attribute the tapestries to Arras, Tournai, or Bruges, but most agree that the set was done somewhere in France. Although the artists are unknown, various theories exist as to their identity, with some art historians claiming that the original cartoon design, as well as the weaving itself, was done by women.

Unlike a comparable set of tapestries, *The Hunt of the Unicorn* (itself a superb work which hangs in the Metropolitan Museum's Cloisters Collection in New York), *The Lady* cycle possesses an almost magical quality of calm stateliness. *The Hunt* sequence is violent, dramatically psychological, and undeniably Christian in its ambience. *The Lady* cycle seems somehow older, more intense even in its understatement, and at once more classical and more "pagan" in tone. To me, *The Lady* set, though not as well-known as *The Hunt*, is filled with what I can only call a more organic sense of grace.

The two most common patriarchal analyses of the Lady-and-Unicorn myth are the Christian (the Unicorn as Christ in divine innocence and the Lady as Mary in virginal purity), or Freudian (the Unicorn as quintessential male, his horn as phallus; the Lady as stereotypical passive female). While both such puerile explanations of the myth certainly have much in common with each other, neither seems to explain the Cluny tapestries. On the contrary, the archetypal dignity of *La Dame à la Licorne*—not to speak of the symbolism both obvious and subtle throughout all six extant panels—exposes such interpretations as pathetically shallow.

The following poem was two years in the writing, during which time, in studying the tapestries and researching their iconography, I discovered that not one character, flower, herb, tree, animal, color, or heraldic symbol was without esoteric significance in a *pre*-Christian religious system. The system reflected was, in fact, Wiccean, redolent with consistent symbolism from matriarchal, goddess-worshiping, "pagan" and nature-faiths. The weavers clearly knew what they were doing. They, together with the poets of their day, had taken upon themselves the task of encoding in their art the message of an earlier age—an age when the flowering of Provençal poetry had paralleled a renaissance of the political and cultural power of women. That had been the era of the magnificent Eleanor of Aquitaine and her daughter the Countess Marie, the age of the Languedoc poets, when the heresy of Mariolatry had so flourished in the Church as to threaten even the primacy of Christ. Woman-reverence: the history and myth of this theme still remained so vivid in European culture that only the Inquisition fires would be sufficient to quench such a memory. Those fires, which began with the Albigensian extirpation in the thirteenth century (when weavers became prime suspects and remained the most steadfast of heretics among the millions killed), were not to cease until the eighteenth century—The Burning Time, it has been called, when all of Europe was engulfed in wave upon wave of religious persecution: the torture and burning of witches and heretics. (I refer the reader to Anna de Koven's *Women in Cycles of Culture* and to Robert Briffault's *The Troubadours* for more background on the Provençal culture, and to Robert Graves' *The White Goddess* for a further explication of the ancient origins of the Lady-and-Unicorn myth, the sacred trees, the Goddess's mirror, etc.)

Despite their fame as works of visual art, the Cluny panels have not been given their due, except in the writings of art historians or in specialized works on tapestry. George Sand did write a romantic essay on the sequence, and Rainer Maria Rilke wrote movingly though briefly of the set in *The Notebooks of Malte Laurids Brigge*. For the most part however, writers have astonishingly enough ignored *The Lady with the Unicorn* tapestries, their history, and their aesthetic implications.

This six-part poem, therefore, was written in awe and love about a great work of art created more than five hundred years ago by, in all likelihood, women. I feel this possibility is strengthened not only by what we know of women's social position in that historical period, but even more by what we can perceive in the tapestries themselves:

certain perspectives, themes, relationships. Whoever the designers and weavers were, though, they understood the female principle. And they were artists. They delineated in patience and complexity a set of late-medieval wall hangings, windows of cloth, one might say, carefully constructed with lyricism, wise humor, and a sense of the tragic, through which we may if we dare, all this time later, gaze—and share a profound vision of the universe.

R.M.
January 1976
New York City

VOICES FROM SIX TAPESTRIES

THE CHOOSING OF THE JEWELS

The Weavers Speak:

From the beginning
there has been one story
surviving all its versions.
We who have lived and still relive its living
here set down what we remember of the pattern—
mere details of clues lost in the execution.

Each of us has brought her own imperfect skill
humbly to this work
so that together our *chansons de toile*
might weave the story through six tapestries
for time to fade and weather stiffen.

We know
how the clearest dyes we blend will age,
bleeding colorless beyond the borders;
we know of edges bound to fray
from centuries of careless hoarding,
possessed by a nobility's delusion.
We use no gold or silver threads, knowing
how other tapestries will be ungrained for hunger,
their strands of metal melted down
to fuel the heat of revolutions.
Silk and wool suffice us, the yarns
looped around our wrists
finespun as manacles
of a devotion self-imposed;
the filaments, like rosaries, uncoiling
rhythmic through our fingers,
although we know eventual edicts on museum walls
will label our work untouchable.

Knowing all this, we labor still—
weaving for the weave's sake, and to trace clues
covered and recovered in the execution
as they unreel themselves.

This matters more to us
than realizing nothing
someday may remain at all—
not even fragments
of the story we have lived
in all its versions,
and still relive,
and here set down.

So it begins.
A slate blue oval island
floats against perspectives of vermilion.
Four mystery trees grow here:
the palm of the year's birth,
the holly of sacrificial passage
and its twin, the royal oak,
and the immortal quince of resurrection.
Each is in bud, leaf, flower, and fruit
at once—all seasons
hub in this eternal place.

The very air, horizonless,
vibrates with creatures:
falcon and ibis
circle the burnt sky.
A goat paws the nearer distance,
arrested in the act of grazing.
Rabbits crouch, startled;
two of them appear to weep.
A lamb nips at a sprig of columbine, not far
from one of the white hounds, red-eared,
who wear ruby collars.
Branches, torn from their trunks, blizzard,

still flowering, through the air:
hawthorne and pomegranate,
cattails, sword lilies—
a *millefleurs* radiance on the loom of space.

The island is carpeted with periwinkle,
yellow flag, woodrose, and violet.
Thistles bed into nests
for field daisies, which brood yoke-hearted
inside broken eggshell petals.
On such a ground they stand:
the animal born of myth,
the woman born of woman.

There, far to the right, beneath the quincetree,
the unicorn supports between uplifted forelegs
a banner; across from him, a lion, rampant,
bears a streamer—both flags unfurl the same insignia:
gules, a band azure, charged with three ascendant crescents.
Between them, in the center of the island,
strung against palm and holly trunks,
floats the Lady's tent: a sapphire bell of satin
flocked with a rain of *yods*, those tongues of fire
which call spirit into matter's transformation.
The tent is lined with watered silk
the color of blanched apricots,
its flaps drawn open ceremoniously
by unicorn hoof and lion paw.

The Lady, clad in gold brocade and scarlet,
stands before this threshhold.
One feather, like a horn, exalts her turban,
surmounting such a face
as only wisdom could empale.

She is attended by a younger woman, slighter,
more simply gowned but still luxuriant
in milder moiré shades of coral,

her hair bound corniform
in imitation of her lady's headdress.
A little dog whose face admits unwhimpering concern
sits eloquently on a damask cushion,
and near the Lady's feet a russet
monkey squats, as if in waiting.

None of the creatures look at one another
in this scene, though some may iterate specific
strands of the entire design
as time unweaves their legend.
But what they say will come too late.
It is beginning:

The Lady is poised above a casket
proffered by her maiden.
The Lady knows some secret,
and its unburdening will be a trial
for which she must be well arrayed.
The casket ripens with jewels harvested
for her to wear as talismans—
but undistracted, she selects
five perfect senses
already mined, weighed, cut, polished, and perfected
for the setting of her body.

It has begun.
Only the unicorn has fixed his amber eyes
upon the Lady's face,
or does he too stare past her—
to the gold-embroidered words that blaze
above her tent's forbidden folds, the legend:
To My One Desire.

Hearing

The Handmaiden Speaks:

Harkening to myself plead silently with her
makes a continual music, a dirge louder
than the gasp of bellows I pump by hand
for the small organ pipes through which she composes
herself, sometimes, like now—
strange melodies, unearthly, always sad—
though whether her playing presumes
to calm herself or me
or to call messages to that wild ox she fancies
I could not say.

Yet we brought her harmonium with us
to this godforsaken island,
and set it up, and still perform together,
she and I, as if in a proper palace courtyard
instead of here, this thicketed indecency
where our sole courtier is a fox
diverted from his ewe, herself a placid audience;
our singular gallant that great hulking lion
who glares and thwacks his tail in rhythm to our song.
My Lady's antlered prince, of course,
he listens all contemplative—I know it,
though I turn my back on him.

Lady, I sing—struck mute by my fear for her—
come Lady, come away, come home.
Lords gone a-hunting should patrol menageries.
This is no place for music, here
where rabbits hiss at jackals
and the heron's shriek imbues the atmosphere.
Come Lady, come away.
This island is not all it seems.
You cannot tame love here,

you cannot plant our moon-emblazoned
standards here, on such a site.

Lady, I sing, I understand, I know you.
I am your fool, your last friend,
your maiden, apprentice to your mysteries.
I will be you yourself someday.
For this alone, I beg you, come away.
Lady, you stand on nettles barefoot,
and beneath your skirt blackberry vines
embrace your ankles—all this concealed
by a velvet serenity of the hem.
I know you, Lady. Come away.

I have heard you at night, past moonset,
clothed in nothing but your lamentation,
and watched, each dawn, your pride rise
like that aigrette you bid me plait
above your forehead, the braid which I myself will wear
no longer. Come home now,
come away.

Lady, how long must we believe in love?
How long labor here, delivering your vision?
What can you bring to bear in such a grove as this?
Whom do you seek beneath hooves, hide, and horn?
Why do you risk scarring your maidenhood,
risk being gored by a leperous apparition?
When will you speak—not sing your wordless lullabies,
but speak? Speak now, to me.
Could all his braying counterpoint your song as I do?
Hear me. How can you bear the pity in my eyes?
Where can you find refuge when I leave you?

Yes, Lady, leave you.
Though I will stay until my heart
grows stunted with the vigil,

knowing that every moment I seem smaller
in your eyes, feeling myself shrink
beyond the possibility of aiding you—
which help you would again refuse.
And then, my sister, I will leave.

I have my own inevitable pilgrimage to travel,
seeking what you have captured.
Deaf to what calls you on your journey,
I have heard, followed, loved
your journeying itself, and you,
mistress, future, you whom I will become—
but in my own time, my own manner.
There must be other means
of capturing what you seek.

You could spare us both, my Lady.
Come, come away, come now.
You almost seem to hear me.
Yet your next note, like an arrow
from your throat's arched bow,
sings along the air, obsessed,
to your one desire.

SMELL

The Lion Speaks:

Tame, you think? Never.
Merely because I sit up, domesticated
as a kitten, waving a pennant
in beggar's paws? Tame, you think?
Merely because this jungle has been cultivated
like a hothouse, bulbs forced to umbrage,
caesarean, before or past their seasons?

Tame like my brother there, the roe
in the thicket, awaiting his initiation?
The beast alone can comprehend the beast.
Not for nothing do both he and I wear shields now,
albeit stamped with the Lady's arms.
Mine, at least, is buckled and barred sinister—
legitimacy's brand denied, her sign
that I will never be adopted as the favorite
nor condemned to etch a silver silhouette
against the holly, like my brother.

He was not always so submissive.
There was a time when his fleet crescent hooves
would print their fury for no mortal sake,
when, with both manes bristling leonine,
he and I would race as equals.
The beast alone can love the beast.
Now he is changed, neck stretched for the bridle.

He will not smell her out
until it is too late for all of us.
How mild she seems:
the face open as a calyx
swaying on her torso's stem.
How tame! How much the gentlewoman she appears,
choosing not that one, no, this one, unblemished,
a fresh carnation from the platter offered

by that sullen maid. This lady has trained herself
to exact the precise bloom she requires
from all that floral surfeit.

Tame, you think? Notice the craft
she weaves into her garland.
How indifferent she appears to other choices,
though marigolds and bluebells
lavish themselves upon the air around her,
though such flowering herbs as cuckoopint and clary
offer her their healing properties;
notice how she rejects as well the basket
munificent with roses on the bench beside her.
Only the monkey, that traitorous beast
devolving to the human,
pities the gratuitous perfume
of a rose found wanting. Fool.

Observe, if you think her tame,
that for the purpose of this wreath she must elect
the flower named for flesh;
that of all the shades available to her
she needs but two:
red, for passion, you assume—or blood.
And white, for purity, you think—or death.
Only the beast can recognize the beast.

Only my still wild instinct can detect the stench
beneath such pungencies. Whatever blossoms
rots. Whatever lives transcends itself
to carrion, and all your oils and unguements
cannot detain the odor of your dying.
Birth, too, reeks as it unswaddles
every chartreuse tendril
fetid with rags of dirt,
or stinks of the compost heap between the legs
where each of us, the baseborn love-child

and the favorite alike,
aspires first this rank air.

Existence on this island
can be tamed only so far, say, as a lamb's
repose, where she lies down temporal
beside the blond bolt of my tail's deathlash—
though every gland beneath her fleece
is redolent with fear,
neophyte of the curled tongue
beckoning through my jaws.

Yet I would devour this totem lamb
solely to understand myself
one such moment of tranquillity.
I would imitate the little ape,
if I could learn such austere expectation.
Oh brother unicorn, I savor your desire
for some connection between life and living.

You think she will initiate this union,
but I, I see you waiting for her garland
to crown your trophied head,
and I can almost know you for another self,
can almost mourn for us—
except some tawny impulse flickers
like a jaundice through my pelt,
and then I lust for nothing but to rend
the cumulous cloud of you
with all my lightning self.
Only the beast can penetrate the beast.

The monkey will desert you toward the end,
the handmaiden betray her lady.
Why must my task be mine? To stay,
expose this process, reveal the site
to any who can read my signals,

alert all who approach it,
and witness for my pains its acrid essence
etherize a sweetness for you, unicorn.
Brother to your beast-body, to her beast-mind,
I must remain, alone beside you both,
the signet of your danger.

Fools, that you think your love
can tame existence.
I know it is the lioness who kills.
I know you, Lady.
I know
your one desire.

Taste

The Monkey Speaks:

I may be a petty scantling
barely noticed in the foreground,
but such a central inconspicuousness
can mellow one's illusions.
At least if I cannot escape observing
nothing will escape my observation.

I realize how the palmtree and the quince
command the island now, together
dwarfing oak and holly
for the first time and the last.
I note the appearance, unexpected, rare,
of a spotted civet, feared by poisonous serpents
not seen as yet about this place.
No longer solitary, I intuit
the presence of a cousin marmoset
who will in turn intuit me.
Philosophical, I compare the posture
of a gabriel hound, severely bred to patience,
with that of the Lady's puppy, a brichon frisé
just as severely bred to helplessness, who cuddles
his silken self into the train-lengths of her gown.
The increase of rabbits interests me,
as does the sly preoccupation of that cougar
nuzzling forget-me-nots.

I relish each ingredient of the scene,
my senses billowing like this sudden wind,
central, invisible,
partaking of each consciousness—
the only permanence here my change.

As the lion, I perceive the unicorn
for the final time: a bitterness
which unfurls vivid as her colors

now clasped around his throat and mine.
As the handmaiden, I am gravely robed
in flint-blue mourning; I half-kneel beside my mistress.
How heavy this chalice is!
But I left it, staggering, for the Lady's absent-
minded plucking of a morsel from its golden depths.
The Lady herself, oh. There I stare out
from beneath the heavier weight of my own garland;
I wear a glove against the claws of a parakeet
perched on my free hand, its wings still spread,
eager to feed. The talons penetrate the cloth,
but I feel nothing yet except an iridescence,
heaviest of all.
And he, the antelope, her conjured wish,
the white hart of her dreamscape forests,
the white center of the fire-tipped roses thorning
the palisade behind her, the white brine
of tears diluted on her lips,
the white rearing of her crescent heraldry
—as him, I look behind me,
a farewell gaze.

But as myself, I have an appetite
in motion between the bestial and humanic,
at once able to foretaste and to recall
how rancid knowledge is,
how cloying innocence.
I know no reason for this process but itself:
the tasting. I call it love—
a furious consummation unconsumable,
consuming all, consummate.

I know the risks better, perhaps,
even than the unicorn or his conjured wish, the Lady.
I can imagine cages more sour to the spirit
than the arbor rising on this island:
the cage that studies the experimental subject,
the cage that is committed to the pet,

the cage that demands survival of the endangered,
the cage that rehabilitates the disobedient and the mad,
the portable cage of nightmare,
the cage of teeth that confines the furred tongue
circling fanatically within,
seeking to express the taste of freedom, which I call love,
beyond the yellow calcium bars.

I can imagine that which I approach in the humanic:
a cacophany of thought already massing in my brain,
cloth shaming my limbs, tools which will cease
to obey my opposable thumb,
speech which will famish my mouth with the unsayable,
and an acquired taste for the eradication
of my own kind and other animals, as well as
soil, air, water—a gourmet of murder.
I know, too, that what I leave behind unsentimentally
is no more noble than any other form of life
on the ellipsis of this island:
the quarry's dread, the predator's self-nausea,
need and survival overwhelming all compassion,
raw blood still pulsing warm between carnivorous jaws,
or even this sharp flavor
of leaves torn ragged from the roots
in fistfuls to be ground alive,
my skull a tomb
that echoes their green thin screaming.
I know there is no pure act possible
in such a place—except for motion, process,
transformation. I call these love.

For in that delicacy of creation
nothing is not impure.
This is one hunger which the collars
we all come to wear cannot contain.
It is perfection's thirst for consciousness.
Its spice refreshes, gingerous,
momentary as the specter

Touch

The Unicorn Speaks:

I feel only her who bears me,
peaceful as an unborn god
among wild orchids, iris, flowering strawberry,
centered and becalmed in her.
I fear that I am less afraid each moment.
We spin toward a compression distant from where
the five-petaled quince uncurls to palm leaves;
here acorns gather in the air
and kernels of holly clot like clouds
before a storm.
The island contracts its boundaries,
sparing no room for fences.
We stand at the world's edge
and our companions leave us
or grow numb, unfeeling what we sense.
Lady, was this your one desire?

Your maiden abandoned you,
who now offer the sole human presence here
amid beaks, claws, and hooves.
She took with her your means of music,
your shelter, your littlest dog,
your vessels of beaten gold, your jewels.
She took with her the streamer, your insignia.
You rally the remaining banner all alone.
It is ponderous. I know, I have borne it.
Yet you balance its gravity with a single hand.
Your lips constrict around no outcry.
Was this the price entailed
for your one desire?

The lion cannot endure it,
he averts his eyes from us—
though he as well as I
now wears your shield, banded and waxed

lunate as my own, legitimate. Is there nothing
you fail to remember or acknowledge, Lady, nothing?
Is all this encompassed by
your one desire?

The other creatures suffer us
from their newfound bondage:
hound, leopard, jackal wear collars now,
torques studded with gems embrazening bright leaves,
the monkey harnessed and chained as well
to a rolling weight almost as heavy
as your standard. A partridge, straying here
in search of her brood, appears transfixed
upon our border. A rabbit darts in fright.
The pulse feels stayed in such a stillness,
as if my heart were past appeasing.
How can this be
your one desire?

Lady, I fear
you are less afraid each moment.
I stand closer to you now,
all four hooves firm as the quarters of a compass
on this contracting ground, rearing no longer.
Your dustgreen velvet train brushes my foreleg,
alive as moss; one fold of the gown
confesses a panel of ermine,
a touch of royalty disguised.
Your unbound hair escapes the crest of your tiara
as rays convey the sun,
to frame a forehead smoother than repose
above eyes old with grief.
You embark, immovable.
There is no possible return.
I lean toward you across immensity,
tranquil as an undead god
straining after wisdom,

all my concentration consecrated.
Was this your one desire?

You have been journeying here forever,
all history your motion.
You conjure me, the consort, the horned god,
assemble me, cohere me, constellate my quickening
through your infinite womb of space.
I have drowsed toward this moment
since your figure, nakedly evolving at the cave's mouth,
eclipsed all else for me where I stood poised—
marble faun, milk yearling, white hind,
ivory roebuck—and felt your grandeur
branching through my brain, transforming me
into the pearl stag young upon the mountain.
Now we are here, where no hills impinge
on a sky blushed numb of stars.
Have we come so far as this to rest?
Was that your one desire?

How still you are, eyes reflecting
a distance I cannot comprehend.
I feel your hand, like a covenant,
bless my brow, invoking its spine, deciduous,
from the cells of memory: an artifactual skeleton of love.
I feel your hand, but cannot tell
whether its pressure would caress me, claim me,
lead me forth, warn me away, protect me,
lift my head for a sword's stroking—
or merely share with me some exquisite intolerable burden
should I now prove worthy.
I cannot tell which,
or whether all of these,
would constitute your one desire.

Only do not remove that touch.
Terror beats its wings around us

and life's green articulations are espaliered
while creatures circle our serenity on leashes.
Yet inexhaustible calm energy spirals
between your crescent fingers and this bone.
Molecules of marble know such a rest, and galaxies,
trembling near one another across immeasurable night.
This is the dream of dreaming we are waking.
This is the repose past hope, delusion, understanding.
This is the space in which my one desire at last
is to dare hear, breathe, taste, and touch,
undreamt till now,
your one desire.

SIGHT

The Lady Speaks:

Oh unicorn, it has begun.
The final mystery, of death and resurrection,
only the holly and the oak may canopy.
I would have spared you this
if it were possible.

The little beasts play innocently now.
They have rushed, cataracting from us,
backward to the edge of blindness—
shields, cloaks, and collars no longer needed
for protection that does not exist.
No birds are left to fly from us.

The lion remains nearest, a patient ensign,
although he will not glance at our embrace.
His eyes, instead, scan all approaches
for those whom he expects,
those who will be drawn here by the focus of that standard
he lofts above the island as a signal
taller even than the chieftan trees.
Its fringed rectangle shimmers faintly over us
like a stiff silk door only now tremoring open
or a portal drawing closed at last, soundless and slow.

Oh lost to me, my tragic guardian of this gate,
my golden cat who smolders to a beacon
with the fever of his vigil—
no less my son for all his burning.
And oh my lovely maiden, lost to me
because she judged my self in her
a weakness, as though I had not known our strength,
as though I did not know escape
to be the first step toward returning,

as though I had not once served such a lady.
I would have spared us all from this
if it were possible.

Oh unicorn, never have you been so close to me,
nestled by my side as if you were a child,
your two great front hooves
settled chastely in my lap.
Your tail flames silver, keratoid
as my own hair, which I myself have braided
to one spire, a sign for you.
The windless current here
has blown both plumes identical.
See, the ritual cloth of gold I wear for you
is lined with crimson velvet.
I have doubled back the outer skirt
so that your hooves may softly lean there.

Never have you been so beautiful to me, oh unicorn.
Not when, as in a visitation, I watched you
gallop free across moon valleys,
tossing shadows from your mane.
Not when I rode you, feeling bare flanks and knees
answer the ripples of your back,
my head bent to your cool body,
the two of us one sinew exuberating speed.
Not when the taste of longing for you
lodged in my palate, a permanent hunger,
or when every breeze haunted my nostrils with your fragrance.
Not even when your hoofbeats sounded louder
than my heart, and your ghost-call whinnied through my nights.
Never have you been so beautiful to me as now.

If I seem weary then, it is because
I have for so long spent my strength,
a beast of burden,
under the whole vast vision of our love,

a weight still lighter than your expectant gaze.
If I seem weary, it is because I undergo
the knowledge of what you yet
have never seen.

Oh unicorn,
the world will make a myth of you and me.
The world will always disbelieve us.
The world will brand me human,
tether my throat with pendants, set me as bait
for your temptation.
The lion, your own purring brother,
will mark my hiding place for them,
accomplishing, he dreams, your rescue at their hands.
My maiden herself, his opposite,
his ally, who knows the way without him—
she will lead them here, oh lost to me,
her fierce love willing even to betray
me for the sake of my salvation, saving instead
merely what she must become.

And you will paw the ground
and then step shyly toward me into a ring of faces
greedy with pain, and all their murderous desire
will penetrate your flesh before my eyes.
My own white hounds will tear my blood,
a cornucopia of hollyberries, from your side,
and men will lead you from me
while women burn incense and number our names in beads.
The world fashions its sacrifices, unicorn,
from such as you and I—
though beasts and men alike
go blind, deaf, and insensate
to your silence, straining toward extinction in their paddock,
or to the shrieks I chant, soon stolen
for adoption in their ceremonies.
How can myths suffer their own reliving?

I have foreseen this, unicorn,
and would have spared you.
If I seem weary then, it is with waiting
that you might behold how I was laden
before this moment—
when I cannot spare you any longer
the spectacle of how the world
makes myths from such as you and I.

But look, I see beyond all this as well,
to a time when we will not be hunted or adored,
because their fear exhausts itself, even as our progress
inexorably strips us of attendants.
And there, like a leap of thought or matter
toward the other's grace, we are transformed,
merged across species—
                          female and male, myth and human,
beast, bird, leaf, fruit, flower,
music and blood and visions
all facets of one jewel, faultless,
within whose rainbow galleries we pulse as prisms,
upon whose crystal walls six tapestries
which tell our story are displayed, a splendor
woven by the hands of women whose *chansons de toile*
knew better than they understood
each thread's relation to every other in this legend.

Look. Visitors pass before us, viewing the tapestries:
That woman weeps in silence at what she recognizes
in my face. The man who stands beside her
feels love branching through his brow.
The one desire, my unicorn, has been that you should see
how, from the first, inevitably,
all this raveled from your eye.

We will be torn from one another and ourselves
to fall like *millefleurs* branches
across the warp and weft of time,

though some dim threads of us are twined forever here—
your hooves on my lap,
my arm, so, lightly resting on your neck,
our separate glances now
one infinite reflection.

Unicorn, I have a mirror in my other hand.
Look in the glass and know what I have always seen:
birth, initiation, consummation, repose, and death,
the five conscious senses, your incandescence,
and my love: these glimpses of the mystery.
There is nothing more, anywhere, ever,
except the myth a world will make of us.

Here is the mirror.
Turn your gaze to what has been my one desire
from the beginning:
that I might behold what you beheld
beholding this,
my one desire.

ABOUT THE AUTHOR

ROBIN MORGAN has been widely acknowledged as a leading poet of the Feminist Movement since the appearance of her first book of poems, *Monster*. She compiled and edited the influential anthology *Sisterhood is Powerful*, and her poetry and prose have frequently appeared in both literary and political journals. A collection of her essays dating from the early 1960's to the present, entitled *Going Too Far*, will be published in 1977. She is currently at work on a verse play, a third collection of poems, and a book of historical fiction on the lives of women accused of witchcraft. She lives in New York City with her husband, the poet Kenneth Pitchford, and their child, Blake Ariel.